JOINING THE DARK SIDE

THE ROLE OF THE
FORENSIC SCIENCE DEFENCE EXPERT

JOINING THE DARK SIDE

THE ROLE OF THE
FORENSIC SCIENCE DEFENCE EXPERT

DAVID SCHUDEL

World Scientific

NEW JERSEY • LONDON • SINGAPORE • BEIJING • SHANGHAI • HONG KONG • TAIPEI • CHENNAI • TOKYO

Published by

World Scientific Publishing Europe Ltd.

57 Shelton Street, Covent Garden, London WC2H 9HE

Head office: 5 Toh Tuck Link, Singapore 596224

USA office: 27 Warren Street, Suite 401-402, Hackensack, NJ 07601

Library of Congress Cataloging-in-Publication Data

Names: Schudel, David, author.

Title: Joining the dark side : the role of the forensic science defence expert / David Schudel.

Description: New Jersey : World Scientific, [2023] | Includes bibliographical references and index.

Identifiers: LCCN 2022017928 | ISBN 9781800612440 (hardcover) | ISBN 9781800612563 (paperback) | ISBN 9781800612457 (ebook) | ISBN 9781800612464 (ebook other)

Subjects: LCSH: Forensic science--Great Britain. | Forensic scientists--Great Britain. | Evidence, Expert--Great Britain.

Classification: LCC HV8073 .S3445 2023 | DDC 363.250941--dc23/eng/20220602

LC record available at https://lccn.loc.gov/2022017928

British Library Cataloguing-in-Publication Data

A catalogue record for this book is available from the British Library.

For any available supplementary material, please visit
https://www.worldscientific.com/worldscibooks/10.1142/Q0367#t=suppl

Disclaimer: The views and opinions in this book are those of the author and not of any employer, agency or professional association associated with him.

Desk Editors: Jayanthi Muthuswamy/Adam Binnie/Shi Ying Koe

Typeset by Stallion Press
Email: enquiries@stallionpress.com

Preface

"So, you're going to the dark side?" he asked me.

That's what they call it. That's what they say when you decide to hang up your lab coat and leave the cosy confines of a prosecution career to work as an 'independent'. At some point, you'll be walking back through the same lab door, but wearing a suit covered by a black cape, breathing heavily, and armed with a clipboard. In other words, you'll be working for the defence.

Most people who say it are joking, but not all. There are those on the 'good' side who really think your goal is to damn the innocent and help keep the guilty out of prison. Perhaps they're scared you'll use all the little secrets you've accumulated at the lab to catch them out. Or perhaps their view is tainted by the few rotten apples who seem to thrive on ego or greed and pose a threat to the wheels of justice, like the scientist who once suggested to me that checking their work would be a waste of time. According to them, their lab's work was so good that no-one could possibly find anything wrong with it.

History tells us differently. Don't get me wrong; there are experts who don't know what they're doing, who are ruthless, arrogant, and egotistical, but they don't all work for the defence. To the contrary, there are several—prosecution experts included—whose feathers finally fell off when they flew too close to the legal sun. (One of the most famous examples of this is the Birmingham Six case, which we'll come to later.) What I mean to say is that if there is ever any doubt, it pays to have someone disconnected from matters and who knows what they're doing to give things a once over, just to make sure the case isn't one of the few that ends in a miscarriage of justice.

The Birmingham Six case is one of the few examples of wrongful conviction to have made the news. The UK has reporting restrictions on cases that haven't gone to trial, and for good reason. What the public remains blissfully unaware of are the numerous cases that die either before a trial starts or on its first day due to half-cooked prosecutions, disconnected thinking, and misunderstood forensics.

I would like to blame it on austerity, which hasn't helped, but the problems have been around for decades. What austerity *has* done is magnify them. It has pushed overworked and underpaid police, Crown Prosecution Service (CPS) and court staff harder and harder, trying to keep cases moving to meet deadlines that aren't realistic. Today, many cases are brought to court prematurely, looking like papier-mâché models of what they would have been 20 years ago; you only need a finger to poke a hole straight through them.

But that's now, and in 1991 we weren't in the grip of austerity. Nor did I wade into a prosecution lab at the start of my career, only to leave it 20 years later to become an independent expert. Nope: I went straight to the Dark Side.

About the Author

David Schudel is currently employed as a forensic science consultant in the UK. He obtained his BSc in chemistry/computer science in 1987, and his PhD in chemistry in 1992, both from the University of Hull. He started work as a forensic scientist in 1991 in the UK, and then the US, Cayman Islands (twice) and back to the UK where he currently resides. Over the years he has been involved in many different types of forensic enquiries and given expert evidence in England, Wales, Scotland, Northern Ireland, Ireland, Massachusetts (US), Cayman Islands and Guyana.

Acknowledgements

Many thanks to Angela Tanzillo-Swarts for her excellent contributions regarding DNA analysis.

Also thank to Sophie Chew for her copyediting skills.

Contents

Jumping in the Dark End

I think we all have a selection of things we are naturally good at. For some, it's sport; for others, it's crafts. For me, it was chemistry. And being a brat.

At 16, my report card was well summarised by the words "suffers from misplaced intellectual arrogance." Even then, I laughed because the teacher had nailed it. How arrogantly misplaced is that? It didn't get much better at 17 and I almost failed my A-levels, with a style reserved for people who, like me, suffer from this terrible affliction. In the end, I scraped through maths and physics, but thankfully did well in chemistry and got into the University of Hull. I studied there until I was 21 and had no idea what I wanted to do next, except that I didn't want to work in a chemistry lab.

This is where everything changed. While talking about the question of my future, a friend casually said, "Why don't you do forensics?" A large penny dropped, and a few months later I found myself at the business end of an interview with the Met.

It was 1987. I was 21, and this was my first job interview. I took the train down to London, which at my age and living in the North East, counted as international travel.

Compared to today, the trains back then were dismal affairs, which might make you wonder just how bad they could have been. (Trust me, you'll never see a sandwich limper than one from a British Rail café. I swear they used to steam them first.)

I got out at King's Cross, into the cloying diesel smoke that filled the station back then, and made my way through the Underground. I remember sitting in a clammy corridor, wearing my silvery-grey suit from the 'there's a reason it's on sale' range at Topman. My name was called, and I walked through a heavy wooden door into a large, bleak room.

If it wasn't for the seriousness of the situation, it'd have looked like I'd walked into a comedy skit. At one end of the room was a lonely chair and, what felt like a hundred metres away, a table with three stern men sitting at it. There was no art or furniture, no bowl of sweets, no bookcase with P.D. James novels on it; even the walls were painted in the shade 'antique left-overs'.

What followed wasn't an interview but a school punishment. I can only assume the Met's method for selecting the best candidate was to see how well they fared during a good old-fashioned beating.

Several questions into the onslaught, I was asked how I would explain gas chromatography to a member of the public. I floundered, stalled and tried to put an answer together, but it stuttered out of me like I was being choked. One of the Conquistadors eventually interrupted me and said, simply and calmly in plummy English, "It's a means by which a mixture of chemicals can be separated into their individual components." At that point, I knew it was over.

After that, I tried a different tactic and did a doctorate, albeit only because I had read that you could get into the Home Office Forensic Laboratory at a higher level if you had one. It seems excessive, I know; worse still, by the time I'd done it, the Home Office had scrapped that system and made their forensic service an Executive Agency. That said, those (and there were several) who told me having a PhD would make me too specialised to get the job I wanted were all wrong. It opened almost every door I tried, plus I got to spend three years playing with liquid nitrogen whilst blowing holes in plastics with lasers. Everyone loves a laser. And liquid nitrogen.

As my PhD research ended and I began writing it up began, I found myself in my hometown of Durham, living with my parents once again and looking for work. My plan was simple: get a job in forensics or join Voluntary Services Overseas (VSO), which is a bit like the Peace Corps.

I had my VSO interview lined up for March 1991. I was excited about the opportunity and had researched life in Africa, where I'd probably end up. You were expected to put in two years abroad, and I figured that as far as my career was concerned, it would make a great interview topic when I came back. But by pure coincidence, I also found out about a company called Keith Borer Consultants (KBC). They did forensic science and were based on the Durham University campus.

On a whim, I walked up wearing a sweatshirt, jeans and baseball boots and stuck my head through the door. It looked more like an office than a lab.

"Do you do forensics?" I asked.

"Yes," replied a boyish-faced man sitting behind a desk at the front. "Why, are you looking for a job?"

"Er, yes," I replied cautiously.

"Leave your CV and we'll be in touch."

They called me back for an interview that week. Two weeks later, I cancelled my VSO interview and started a forensic career in sunny Durham.

I had no idea what to expect, let alone any idea that there was a dark side and I was on it, but I sure was excited. I even spent my first day helping to put down new carpet tiles with glee (not what I was expecting, but that didn't matter). Within a few days, I was sliding a sled down a makeshift tile floor to assess how slippery it was when wet; within a few months I was pulling women's underpants off someone to see how they tore compared with a pair from an alleged rape case. Two years in, I had electrocuted myself, almost set fire to the bathroom, singed my eyebrows, and tried not to shoot Dr. Borer by accident. Welcome to forensic science.

If you ever wanted to meet a mad scientist, Dr. Keith Borer was as good as they come. Tall and gangly, with a slight paunch, he wore dark-rimmed glasses and had bright, inquisitive eyes that never seemed to rest. His grey-white hair seemed to grow sideways around his head, leaving a bald crown on top. He spoke rapidly, often changing subjects without warning, as his mind was always processing multiple things at once. As eccentric as he seemed, very little escaped his attention.

Dr. Borer's philosophy was to always hit with a straight bat. In other words, he called it how he saw it, whether the client liked it or not. Even the solicitors who were incensed by our candid reports about their clients would end up coming back years later, after having been roasted in court for relying on a pay-to-say charlatan in expert's clothing. Truth is the kind of peg on which you can hang any business.

Having previously risen through the highest ranks of the chemistry industry, Dr. Borer came at forensic issues with a very different approach. In his view, one of the flaws of the forensic system back then was that many defence experts were former Home Office staff: they had all been trained in the same way, and were therefore more likely to make the same mistakes as well as less likely to criticise their former colleagues (an example of cognitive bias, which we'll come to later).

The head of our main business rival, Forensic Access, held the opposite view. Her name was Angela Gallop, and she was a highly experienced former Home Office employee. To her, in order to be a forensic scientist, one had to be properly trained—in other words, by the Home Office. Dr. Borer's retort to this was always the same: "That's exactly my point!"

Dr. Borer's open mind and willingness to look at problems was a philosophy we all embraced. It was also, I suspect, the reason why he was routinely asked to look at the defence in terrorism cases, including Irish Republican Army (IRA) prosecutions. At the time, the IRA was still active, and undertaking work on behalf of those arrested on IRA terrorism charges wasn't for the faint-hearted. Dr. Borer was often stopped by the police while driving back from the airport. We suspected the office was searched in the middle of the night at least once, and any package that arrived unexpectedly was treated with a great deal of caution. But every person is entitled to a defence, regardless of what they are charged with. After all, the Crown sometimes gets it wrong.

In one case—the name of which I sadly can't recall—the defendant spent 12 years in jail after being found guilty of making around 1,000 bomb timers for the IRA. The timers were small, disposable and had no safety catches on them. The defendant insisted that a Middle Eastern government had commissioned him to make the timers for use in battlefield simulations (e.g. to let off smoke bombs), but for some reason this allegation was never investigated. He maintained his innocence the entire time he was in jail and pursued his appeal even after he had been released.

Dr. Borer's approach to the case was simple: why would the IRA need 1,000 bomb timers? If you added up every bomb the IRA had ever set off, it still wouldn't reach 1,000. You don't need to be an expert to state the obvious, but sometimes that's exactly what we do. The defendant was found not guilty on appeal after having already served his entire 12-year sentence.

My first case wasn't so newsworthy. Picture the scene, circa 1991: a barely-lit churchyard, where one Mr. Smith is walking his dog late at night. He hears a noise in the gloom and sees someone scrambling on the church roof, stealing the lead. He shouts and rushes to call the police from a payphone, during which time the figure runs off.

The police bring in a trained dog to search for the thief. It picks up a trail and the dog courses through the dark church grounds and into some nearby fields, where there is a large pond. The dog launches itself into the air and crashes into the pond, right on top of a young man immersed in the water with his mouth just above the surface. He jumps up and shouts at the officer, "It's a fair cop!"

At least, that's what the officer claimed. According to the young man, he actually said, "Get the dog off!"

The young man denied any theft, though he couldn't give a reasonable explanation for why he was lying in a pond a few hundred yards from the church at midnight. The police sent his clothing for testing at the Home Office Forensic Science lab at Wetherby, where it came back positive for traces of lead on the jeans. I was asked to check the findings.

I was nervous to say the least. I had to meet a seasoned forensic scientist at their lab, examine the jeans and conduct my own test for lead. I made up the chemicals in advance, tested them before I left and arrived at Wetherby an hour later.

The expert, a tall, quiet woman in her 30s, had auburn hair and slightly cautious eyes. We didn't say much, so I cracked on with opening the evidence bag and took out the jeans. To say they had traces of lead on them was an understatement: I could almost stand them up and use them as an X-ray apron. You could feel the weight of the metal, which had formed a thick grey layer on the seat and the front of each leg like it had been hand-painted there.

I got my chemicals out and did the test, which came back a resounding positive. At that point, I heard an exhalation behind me and turned my head.

"It's such a relief when you get the same result," said the expert. It hadn't occurred to me that she was as nervous as I was. I learned a lesson that day: for the most part, we're all just scientists in it together.

Cognitive Bias, Context and Forensics

Finding lead on a pair of jeans is representative of most of the work we do as defence experts. It's belt-and-braces; the final external quality check. If we agree with Crown's report, then from our perspective, that's the end of it.

However, even when we *do* agree, our work is not without value. Counsel might use our report to try (often, after previous unsuccessful attempts) to convince the defendant to reassess their guilty plea options, thus saving the taxpayer tens of thousands in trial costs. Even if that fails, the report can still provide some ammunition for cross-examination.

The defence is not obligated to serve our reports, which unfortunately gives some prosecution experts the impression that defence experts are basically troublemakers who always disagree with them. In reality, that's not what happens: at an educated guess, we agree with the Crown in around 75% of our cases, and in another 20% the concerns are minor. Only around 5% have serious problems. But since prosecution experts only ever see our reports when there's something that needs to be said, they never see the 75–95% which don't have any real issues, making it appear that we're always causing trouble.

This is an example of *cognitive bias*.

The Oxford English Dictionary has various definitions of 'bias', one of which is "[I]nclination or prejudice for or against one person or group, especially in a way considered to be unfair."[1] This recognition that bias is commonly held to be "unfair" reflects how its connotations are generally negative; in conversation, you can rarely be biased in a good way. For example, if you own an Austin Tippex and say to someone, "I think

---

[1] Concise Oxford English Dictionary, 12th edn. (Oxford University Press, 2011).

they're the best car, but then I'm biased!," what does that mean? The subtext is really that the Austin Tippex isn't that good, but I've glossed over its bad points because, well, I'm biased.

Cognitive bias (also called subconscious bias) is both natural and unintentional. You can mitigate its effects, but it can't be completely removed. And even if you can reduce its impact in one area, you might simply shift your bias to something else without realising it.

For these reasons, it is vitally important that cognitive bias can be discussed openly. It is also the reason why I find it massively disappointing that the people who developed the construct of cognitive bias (or, at least, applied it to forensics) decided to label it as such. The negative implications of 'bias' automatically set up any conversation about its effects to fail, and people to instinctively reject the very idea they may have fallen victim to (which, ironically, is an example of cognitive bias). It should have been called something less emotive, such as 'subconscious preferences'—which is really what it is.

Cognitive bias is a hot topic right now. A cognitive bias training programme for government ministers was recently scrapped after a research paper found that it did not materially change people's behaviour,[2] but the concept itself is nothing new.

In 1620, Francis Bacon wrote (as translated from Latin):

> "*The human understanding, when any proposition has been once laid down (either from general admission and belief, or from the pleasure it affords), forces everything else to add fresh support and confirmation; and although most cogent and abundant instances may exist to the contrary, yet either does not observe or despises them, or gets rid of and rejects them by some distinction, with*

---

2   J. Lopez, *Unconscious Bias Training* (Statement UIN HCWS652), UK Parliament (15 December 2020). Available at https://questions-statements.parliament.uk/written-statements/detail/2020-12-15/hcws652.

violent and injurious prejudice, rather than sacrifice the authority of its first conclusions."[3]

This is as true now as it was then.

We believe what we want to believe. Although operating with an open mind is the ideal, all of us are bound to a greater or lesser degree by our existing beliefs, preferences, ego, education, experience, socioeconomic standing, and so on.

Bacon talks about these in terms of the "four idols" of human understanding: the Idols of the Tribe, the Idols of the Den, the Idols of the Market and the Idols of the Theatre. Each of these affects our ability to accurately deduce the world around us.

> **Idols of the Tribe** are the problems of being human. We rely on our senses to take the outside world and process it internally, but in doing so, "the human mind resembles those uneven mirrors which impart their own properties to different objects."[4] Much like a two-dimensional object cannot see three dimensions, we cannot look at ourselves from the outside. Every person is entirely processing the world around them from within.

> **Idols of the Den** are problems which arise from differences in our individual, subjective experiences. Every person comes from a different background, holds different beliefs, and has had different experiences.

> **Idols of the Market** are problems arising from the use of language, where "*men converse by means of language, but words are formed at the will of the generality, and there arises from a bad*

---

[3] F. Bacon, *Novum Organum: New Instrument* (Anodos Books, 2019 [1620]).

[4] Ibid.

and unapt formation of words a wonderful obstruction to the mind."[5] In other words, poor language is a cause of weaknesses in human understanding. Even when the same words are used, there can still be differences in how they are interpreted from person to person. We often see this in forensic science, when expressions like 'in the vicinity of a crime scene' are used with no definition of how big said vicinity is (something we'll come to later).

Idols of the Theatre are problems due to thoughts that have come from "*peculiar systems of philosophy, and…the perverted rules of demonstration*," creating fictitious worlds with little basis in fact. These are beliefs that have been created out of superstition, anecdotal evidence, or experiments with very little data. An example of this is how, in 2011, the Irish Coroner's Court ruled that a death had been caused by "spontaneous human combustion."[6]

Looking at what Bacon said 400 years ago is useful because forensic science remains bound and beset by the same problems as science was back then.

Let's say I start a story by telling you, "A man walks into a bar." Your mind will automatically start to fill in the image. You'll picture a bar, likely one you have been to, and you'll picture a man, who might be someone you know.

If I then tell you that the man walks up to the bartender and says, "Give me some money," you'll start to imagine what is going on. Without prompting, your mind will create a story based on the information I am telling you, mixed with your own subjective views on the subject.

---

[5] Ibid.

[6] J. Fallon, 'Court Finds Pensioner's Death in Fire Caused by Spontaneous Combustion', *The Irish Times* (23 September 2011). Available at https://www.irishtimes.com/news/court-finds-pensioner-s-death-in-fire-caused-by-spontaneous-combustion-1.606542.

Now, what if I tell you that the bartender is a woman? How many of you imagined a man in that role? How does the change in gender affect how you think or feel about the situation? Is it more sinister or less? What if I tell you the man is the bartender's husband, and that he wanted the money to buy some steak to cook for dinner that night but forgot his wallet…?

Yes, it's contrived, but my point is that this is a book about forensic science, and horrible things happen in forensic science. All the same, stories may seem more sinister than they actually are because of the context they are being told in.

As a story unfolds, your mind produces a version of what it thinks is going to happen. Similarly, when witnesses recount an observation, they might subconsciously add on to what they observed or heard because their mind can no longer distinguish what they actually saw from the version of events in their head. In the worst cases, the latter can even replace the former.

Since our world is very much guided by what we see, it's no surprise how fundamental eyewitness evidence is to the criminal justice system. The human eye is our main port of call when it comes to collecting information about the world around us, though I wonder: at what cost to our other senses?

If dogs could talk, I imagine they would not only describe what they saw, but what they heard and smelled as three equally important streams of data comprising a memory. A human might say they thought they saw a person standing in the bushes; a dog might say they saw a human, but as there was no human smell or human-specific sounds, it couldn't actually have been a person there.

Eyewitness accounts tend to rely on just that: the eye. In line with Bacon's Idols of the Tribe, the eye is part of the "uneven mirror" that drops images into our brain, potentially compromising the accuracy of a memory from the start. This can be due to shock, viewing conditions (such as lighting and distance), the duration of an incident, competing distractions (such as a screaming child), and the viewer's own prejudices and state of mind.

That isn't the end of it. Unlike digital cloud systems, where images stay the same once saved, memories can change while in 'storage'. In the case of traumatic events, the memories might be revisited over and over, with some parts considered in detail and others added on from things like news coverage or other people's accounts of the event. By the time a case reaches trial, the final recall of a witness can be very different from how an incident was first perceived.[7]

Unfortunately, the criminal justice system has no control over these conditions and variables. Unless there is a means of solidly verifying the accuracy of a memory, the jury must then consider whether they believe the eyewitness or not.

In cases where there is no other significant physical evidence, trials can proceed provided eyewitness accounts retain their credibility. If a person gives evidence with conviction, adamant that their memories are the truth, their confidence usually comes through regardless of whether their version of events actually happened.

Take the following case from the United States. A spate of cheque forgeries in the state of Massachusetts led Inspector Conboy of the Boston Police Department to mount a hunt for the perpetrator. One October, he was lucky enough to receive a bounced cheque from a merchant with the name of Herbert Andrews on it. It turned out to be a real name, and Andrews was taken to the station, photographed, fingerprinted, and charged with 40 offences. Andrews pleaded his innocence, with supporting testimony from his father, but the Inspector maintained that he had never made a mistake in over 40 years. At this point, you can probably guess how things turned out.

[7] T.D. Albright, 'Why Eyewitnesses Fail', *Proceedings of the National Academy of Sciences* 114(30) 7758–7764 (2017). Available at https://doi.org/10.1073/pnas.1706891114.

As a result of the investigation, an identity parade with the witnesses who had received the bad cheques was organised. Many of them identified Andrews, but the testimonies of those who did not were not recorded. (Of course, if the police ask you to come in for such an exercise, you might reasonably expect that one of the persons in the line-up is the real suspect.) In the end, 17 witnesses took the stand and identified Andrews on oath. He was found guilty on all 17 counts.

The trouble was that the forgeries continued even *after* Andrews began serving his time. Eventually, a separate investigation identified the culprit as one Earle Barnes, who admitted to forging all the cheques. The two men were several inches apart in height and had no physical resemblance. Thankfully, Andrews was released.

This was in 1914.[8] You might think something like this wouldn't take place today, but witnesses' powers of recall are no different from what they were back then; it's not like the human brain has changed. I am not talking about deliberately misleading the court or lying. What I am referring to is, in essence, an honest mistake: a witness may believe in their heart that they are recounting something correctly, and can maintain that conviction even if their account isn't true. Cognitive bias is present in everything we think or do, and plays a part in how memories are formed and stored.

In an article for the *Proceedings of the National Academy of Sciences of the United States of America* (PNAS),[9] Albright argues that the risk is greatest with eyewitness evidence when you have a combination of *uncertainty, bias and confidence.*

- **Uncertainty:** Uncertainty can be generated when a memory is created. Examples of conditions that create inaccurate memories can include instances where an encounter was brief, took place in the

[8]   E.M. Borchard, *Convicting the Innocent: Sixty-Five Actual Errors of Criminal Justice* (Yale University Press, 1932).

[9]   T.D. Albright, 'Why Eyewitnesses Fail', *Proceedings of the National Academy of Sciences* 114(30) 7758–7764 (2017). Available at https://doi.org/10.1073/pnas.1706891114.

dark, or involved persons unknown to the eyewitness. Once a memory has been formed, it can be very hard to displace without overwhelming evidence to the contrary, such as closed-circuit television (CCTV) footage.

Let's say you are an eyewitness to a hit-and-run. The accident is over in seconds and the area in which it happens is poorly lit. You *think* the car involved is yellow, but you're not sure as it all happened so quickly.

- **Bias:** The police have an idea of who the suspect might be, but unintentionally feed you information that affects your memory and observations.

When being interviewed, you say that you *think* the car was yellow, but you're not 100% sure. The detective says, "Are you sure it wasn't a red car?," and you concede that it *could* have been. However, the nuances of that conversation—along with the expression of uncertainty and any body language that accompanied it—are lost in the eventual police report, which simply says, "Eyewitness saw a red car."

- **Confidence:** You later see a news report that a person 'known to the police' had been in the area in a red car, which reinforces your (amended) memory.

A year later, on the witness stand, you testify that the car was red, when in fact initially you thought it was yellow. What comes across is a level of confidence that does not reflect your initial uncertainty.

Despite the repeated issues with eyewitness evidence, it remains as fundamental—and as vulnerable—in criminal matters to this day.

Consider this example from a real case, which occurred a few years ago:

A mother of three woke up in her lounge to find the sofa on fire. She fled to the neighbour's house for help, leaving her three children asleep upstairs. When the fire service arrived and asked her what had happened, she said that she didn't know: she had been asleep on the sofa and woke up because "her feet were hot." (The children were rescued by a neighbour.)

Recalling what we discussed about eyewitness evidence, at this stage, the cause of the fire is unknown, and the mother is technically an eyewitness. Her account does not rely on something that she saw, but something that she *felt*—namely, that her feet were hot.

Now, I would argue this was likely a true statement. Although people tend to lie or be mistaken about things they can see or imagine easily, like colours, locations, actions, and objects, they don't normally lie about smells and sensations. Having "hot feet" is a detail you would only mention if you had actually felt it.

An inspection of the scene showed that the fire had come up from the back and behind the sofa. If the woman had been asleep on it with her head to the other end, her feet would have been toasted from the springs upwards. The early eyewitness account therefore matched the physical evidence.

Despite this, a preliminary fire investigation done that same day determined the cause as arson, but neither the investigation nor a further report were completed.

As a result of this preliminary finding of arson, the mother was no longer treated as an eyewitness, but was interviewed by the police as a suspect. When asked how she thought the fire might have started, she suggested that it might have been an incense burner. However, it couldn't have been, as the incense burner was found in the kitchen, and the police used this answer to say she had lied during the interview.

But *had* she lied? Was this the deliberate misdirection of a guilty arsonist, or a mother who knew she was innocent but was starting to realise the police thought she had done it? She was looking at being sentenced to jail and having her children taken from her. What do you do in such a situation? Do you shut up—and then be accused of not answering the police's questions—or do you panic and try to help by thinking of something that might have started the fire—only to be accused of lying?

One subconscious belief behind the case was that it couldn't truly have been an accident, as no mother would leave her children in a house that was on fire. But that's cognitive bias for you: it's a belief, and whether you agree with it or not depends on your own life experiences (recall Bacon's Idols of the Den).

I've seen people do the oddest things in reaction to a fire or a traumatic incident. One person chose to run out through a burning corridor (and sadly died as a result) rather than stay in their ground floor flat–which was untouched by the fire–or even leave via a window in their bedroom. I know of a young girl who fell down a metal ladder, tearing a hole in her leg. When she screamed, her mother came, saw the injury, then turned and ran for help, leaving her daughter lying there. That made me wonder about our aforementioned mother of three. Did she cause the fire, or did she just panic and run?

Moreover, the case had been driven by the opinion that the fire was a result of arson, despite this being only a finding from a preliminary investigation. The decision seemed to have been made quite early on, which then clouded any subsequent assessment. It was only later that further work revealed the possibility of an electrical failure from a wire under the sofa, which supported what the eyewitness first said: that she woke up because her feet were hot.

Another detail—which I deliberately didn't mention above—was that the mother had mental health issues. I left this out because it might have tainted your consideration of the case. Stereotypes can prejudice us as to who is likely to be innocent or guilty.

Most cases don't rely solely on eyewitness accounts but a mixture of evidence, some of which can be more reliable than others. The actual time of a call to the emergency services (as retrieved from call logs) is considered reliable, but not the time a witness says they called. If the witness' timing is out by, say, five minutes, it can make a massive difference to the interpretation of a case.

In one incident, a young man with no criminal history was arrested because a neighbour was adamant that he had been at the scene at around 10:00PM. The young man claimed he had actually been there an hour earlier with the police, at 9:00PM, but the neighbour said he knew the young man had returned at 10:00PM because a TV show he was watching had just started at the time.

The neighbour was in his 50s and adamant about the timing of the sighting. He had a routine: he would make tea, eat a light supper, and watch his favourite show, which started at 10:00PM. He said he knew the young man was there because he saw him out of his window, and when he looked at the TV, his show was about to start.

All of this was true except one detail: the show had actually started at 9:00PM. I can only assume that the reason why no-one thought to check such a simple fact came down to the witness's sheer confidence. While Google didn't exist at the time (this took place in 1992), a copy of the *Radio Times*, a weekly magazine which listed the timings of all public TV shows, was produced in court. The neighbour was asked to turn to the correct page and read out the time of the show. There was an audible inhalation of shock from the jury as the prosecution's case fell apart: what their star witness had actually seen was the young man attending the scene with a police officer a full hour earlier.

It was an honest mistake by an eyewitness who was utterly sure of what they had seen. At the half-time point of the trial (when the prosecution rests their case and the defence begins theirs), the judge calmly asked the prosecutor, "Counsel, what has happened to your case?" The prosecutor shuffled some papers and replied with a polite smile, "I don't know, your Honour." And that was that.

Let's consider a more up-to-date example. A police officer in a planned undercover operation was conducting surveillance from his vehicle.

He noted that the target car drove past with only a woman driver. The car went up a side road, came back, turned and drove out of the officer's field of sight. Within a minute, other police officers stopped the car, but this time, there were two people in it. The inference was that the driver had collected the other person from the side road, but the suspect said this wasn't true and he had been in the car the whole time.

In order to support the officer's eyewitness account, the Crown produced cell site analysis (CSA) evidence. CSA examines the use, movement, and general location of a cellphone by looking at which cell towers it was using at particular times. Most cell towers send out an area of coverage a third of a circle wide, like a giant lighthouse beam, and can travel for miles. To put it simply, when a cellphone is used, the mobile phone company logs the time and cell tower used, which can be interpreted to get an idea of where the cellphone was at that moment.

Imagine two cellphones travelling together in a car for several miles. If both are in use, you would expect the cell towers to correspond to the movements of the car, but if the towers are in very different locations, then by inference, the phones could not have travelled together, which is what the Crown said the data showed.

That would have been fine—except that it wasn't true. The cell site evidence had been misinterpreted and was actually broadly consistent with both phones moving together. The logical inference from this is that the officer's eyewitness account was probably wrong, and conditions such as poor lighting, distractions (like focusing on the driver) or the difficulty of conducting surveillance from a moving car might have contributed to the confusion.

However, rather than taking this new information and examining its implications—including the possibility of a genuine error by the officer—the prosecution decided to keep the officer's statement, and said that they weren't going to rely on the cell site evidence. They did not explain why the cell site evidence was being withdrawn when it was previously heralded as supporting the officer's claim.

Technically, the Crown is under a legal duty to the court to report anything that might undermine the prosecution's case or assist the defence's.[10] In this case, it was left to the defence to raise the issue. In the end, the point was conceded.

Beyond eyewitness evidence, some types of forensic evidence are more prone to cognitive bias issues as their data or observations are uncertain by nature. Cell site analysis is one of these, as the potential range it gives for where a phone has been can be up to several square miles in size. Unfortunately, this can get lost in reports relating to the evidence.

Take the expression 'the phone was in the vicinity' of a crime, which is often bandied about. A lay person might imagine this means the phone was just around the corner from the scene. In fact, it refers to the entire area covered by the cell tower in use, which could be 12 kilometres or more in rural areas and up to around one kilometre in London.

Harking back to Bacon's Idols of the Market, the Forensic Science Regulator (FSR) guidelines warn against using such terms without defining them,[11] but no set definitions exist, and it is often left to the writer to make up their own. It is common to read things like:

- "The phone was used in the vicinity of the burglary," with "the vicinity" defined as being "within 500 metres of the property."

- "The phone was used in the vicinity of the burglary that night." No definition is provided of how big said vicinity might be or what time it was used during the night. The cell is a mile from the burglary and pointing in the opposite direction.

---

[10] Criminal Procedure and Investigations Act 1996. Available at https://www.legislation.gov.uk/ukpga/1996/25/contents.

[11] Forensic Science Regulator, *Codes of Practice and Conduct Appendix: Digital Forensics—Cell Site Analysis FSR-C-135* (September 2020). Available at https://assets.publishing.service.gov.uk/government/uploads/system/uploads/attachment_data/file/918946/135_FSR-C-135_Cell_Site_Analysis_Issue_2.pdf.

- "The phone was in the vicinity around the time of the assault." It was used in that area—but four hours earlier.

- "Surveys show that the cell used was detected in the vicinity of the property at the relevant time," but the *sequence* of cells used shows that the phone must have been passing through the area, as the next cell tower is half a mile away and the one after that even further.

And it goes on. Loose language like "in the vicinity" or "consistent with" is discouraged because it inspires a false sense of confidence in the data, but it still finds its way into cases.

Just as uncertainty, bias, and confidence can result in errors in eyewitness evidence, the same is also true of expert witnesses. Cell site analysis is uncertain at its core, but add bias in the form of language like "in the vicinity" and you end up with misleadingly confident statements about the movement of a phone at a given time. Moreover, the language of cell site analysis can be compounded by the breakdown in the distinction between a phone and who is using it: although CSA concerns the movement of a phone, once a phone is believed to belong to someone, its movements are often equated with movements of that person.

For example: 07xxxx567 is believed to be involved in a robbery. Cell site analysis then looks at the movement of the phone. The police attribute that phone number to Schudel because he has a contract with Vodafone for that number and Schudel is arrested.

What happens is that the line between what the evidence factually supports (i.e. the movement of the phone number) is conflated with Schudel's movements. '07xxxx567 was in Durham that night' becomes 'Schudel was in Durham that night'. The distinction is subtle, but unless Schudel accepts that this was his phone *and* he was the one using it that night, it is a matter for the jury to consider, rather than to presume they are one and the same.

One area where Bacon's Idols of the Market and Idols of the Tribe have endured the longest is fingerprint comparison. Fingerprints have been accepted as a means of identification the world over, based on the notion that everyone's fingerprints are different. This is founded on a large and evolving body of evidence, but there are also people who do not have fingerprints (a condition known as adermatoglyphia). The notion that everyone has different fingerprints, is, therefore, untrue.

This is an example of cognitive bias that has become so entrenched that there are a few families without fingerprints around the world who are now effectively exiled from travelling to many countries.[12] This is one of the biggest problems in science: the belief that what we know at a single moment in time is correct.

In fairness, aside from that exception, I think we can all agree that when people *do* have fingerprints, those fingerprints are different. But forensic fingerprint comparison is not actually about looking at people's fingers. It is about comparing a *mark* made by a finger (often of varying quality, possibly made in haste or on a poor surface) to a reference mark made by a finger that may or may not even be complete (particularly if the finger was not inked or scanned properly).

In other words, when it comes to comparing *fingerprint marks*, not everyone is different; some marks will appear to be the same even if they are from different people. This is a critical distinction, but one that has historically been lost in the world of fingerprint comparisons, thanks to over-confident statements like "I am of no doubt that this fingerprint mark was made by Mr. X." For decades, such bold statements have become common in this type of evidence, but they should never have been allowed in the first place. Research and high-profile Court of Appeal cases, like *R v. Smith*[13] and *R v. McKie*,[14] have shown that false positive identifications *do* occur.

---

[12] For a discussion of this phenomenon and its associated problems, see: B. M. Sabbir, 'The Family with No Fingerprints', *BBC News* (26 December 2020). Available at https://www.bbc.co.uk/news/world-asia-55301200.

[13] *R v. Smith* (2011) EWCA Crim 1296.

[14] P. McNeill and Others, *Justice 1 Committee Report—Inquiry into the Scottish Criminal Record Office and Scottish Fingerprint Service*, Scottish Parliament Paper 743 (2007). Available at https://archive.scottish.parliament.uk/business/committees/justice1/reports-07/j1r07-03-vol1-00.htm.

Ultimately, cognitive bias isn't just a problem with eyewitnesses, certain types of evidence, or individual expert interpretations. It is also a systemic problem which affects the criminal justice system in many ways—and is often a factor in cases where defence experts get involved.

Types of Cognitive Bias

The most pervasive and destructive form of cognitive bias exists at an institutional level. Many readers will be familiar with recent examples of entrenched racism and sexism, particularly in government organisations, where problems were driven not by individual bias but by systemic problems which resist easy resolution.

Expressions like 'You can't teach an old dog new tricks' reflect the subconscious belief that it's not worth trying to change people. Science is no different, and history has many examples where institutional bias has clouded open-minded thinking. One well-known example is Galileo Galilei, who showed that Earth revolves around the Sun. The Church believed the opposite (i.e. that everything revolved around the Earth), and Galilei was found guilty of heresy. He ended up living the later part of his life under what was essentially house arrest.

Another classic example is the discovery of the platypus. Although a dried pelt and bill had been sent back to the UK from Australia to be studied, for some time thereafter, scientists continued to doubt whether the specimens were real.[1]

We tend to think that we have overcome many of the obstacles impeding scientific progress, and joke about times gone by and how foolish people were back then. We don't know, however, what will be said hundreds of years from now about how we do things today. You only need to look at current scientific issues, such as global warming, pollution, over-population, disease control, and the depletion of the ozone layer, to see the varied, conflicting views wrapped up in a mixture of fact, myth, and bias (both deliberate and subconscious). Four hundred years from now, scholars will still be quoting Francis Bacon's observation that the

---

[1] B.K. Hall, 'The Paradoxical Platypus', *BioScience* 49(3) 211–218 (1999). Available at https://doi.org/10.2307/1313511.

meditations, speculations and theories of mankind are "a kind of insanity, only there is no one to stand by and observe it."[2]

Forensic science is no freer from the shackles of institutional bias than any other human discipline, and care must be taken when accepting or rejecting the status quo as being the right way of doing something. There is no overarching consumer warning on our current forensic guidance that says, "Be careful, some of this might be completely wrong, but we won't know for another 100 years." What we must be aware of is that any of the existing and proposed systems dealing with forensic science will have various entrenched cognitive biases, and this, in large part, drives the need for defence experts.

Writers and researchers have identified numerous types of cognitive bias. For example, a book by Musashi names 25 forms,[3] and one doctoral thesis by Wright lists over 100,[4] but I will refer generally to the Forensic Science Regulator's (FSR's) 96-page guidance on the subject.[5]

The FSR guidance starts with the basic premise that cognitive bias is part of human nature and is similarly present in the criminal justice system, with far-reaching consequences. It states:

> "Simply because there is a risk of a cognitive bias does not imply that it occurs. The problem is that as it is a subconscious bias it is unlikely that an individual will know either way and therefore it is wise that all practitioners understand the issue and take proportionate steps to mitigate against it."[6]

---

[2] F. Bacon, *Novum Organum: New Instrument* (Anodos Books, 2019 [1620]).

[3] K. Musashi, *The 25 Cognitive Biases: Understanding Human Psychology, Decision Making & How to Not Fall Victim to Them* (CreateSpace Independent Publishing Platform, 2016).

[4] J.F. Wright, *The Origin of Cognitive Biases: A Behavioural Approach to Risk Management* (PhD Project, Oslo Metropolitan University, 2018).

[5] Forensic Science Regulator, *Cognitive Bias Effects Relevant to Forensic Science Examinations FSR-G-217* (2020). Available at https://assets.publishing.service.gov.uk/government/uploads/system/uploads/attachment_data/file/914259/217_FSR-G-217_Cognitive_bias_appendix_Issue_2.pdf.

[6] Ibid.

(Of course, if someone is conscious of this but acts anyway, that's just called 'bias'.)

The FSR has promoted quality assurance through awarding accreditation to ISO 17025 or ISO 17020, which are international standards for testing and surveying. Any method accredited to one of these standards is assessed by an external review body, the United Kingdom Accreditation Service (UKAS). The requirement doesn't just apply to laboratories, but to all areas of forensics (except medical), including crime scenes, fingerprint comparisons, digital forensic analysis and so on.

Having an external party check your organisation's methods and procedures is a good thing. It keeps people attuned to and focused on quality adherence, and clients tend to trust your work.

Paradoxically, this can also result in what I call "accreditation bias," where the client believes their report is reliable and therefore better than a non-accredited report, especially under an adversarial court system. If an expert for an accredited lab gives bad evidence and a non-accredited expert tries to shut it down, who will the court side with? Being accredited can actually contribute to a subconscious bias effect where the accuracy of evidence is left unquestioned.

At a large-scale level, the Randox Scandal showed how unscrupulous individuals can still operate under a veneer of trust through accreditation.

I won't go into too much detail, but two Randox scientists were arrested for manipulating results. The scandal broke in 2017, and by December 2018, over 40 drug driving convictions relying on Randox reports had been quashed. Unfortunately, by August 2019, 10,500 samples that needed to be retested by other companies had still not been completed.[7]

---

[7] L. Dearden, 'More than 40 Drug Driving Convictions Overturned in Police Probe over 'Data Manipulation' at Forensics Lab', *Independent* (6 December 2018). Available at https://www.independent.co.uk/news/uk/crime/drug-driving-convictions-overturned-randox-testing-laboratory-manchester-data-manipulation-police-a8671286.html.

Technically, at its root, the Randox scandal isn't an example of cognitive bias. This was actual bias on the part of a toxicology lab responsible for tens of thousands of criminal samples, including drug driving, sexual assault, violent crimes, and unexplained deaths. But Randox was an accredited lab, and this aptly demonstrates that accreditation does not guarantee quality. At the end of the day, individuals—especially if working in groups—can circumvent methods and produce flawed forensic evidence under the supportive banner of accreditation, and their reports will carry a degree of trust for the same reason.

The UK is not alone in this. The US case of *Commonwealth of Massachusetts v. Annie Dookhan* deserves a mention. In August 2012, officials in the state of Massachusetts closed the Hinton State Laboratory after it was discovered that Dookhan, an employee, had been falsifying drug reports from 2003 to 2011. She eventually pleaded guilty to 27 charges and was sentenced to three years in jail.[8]

How could this happen in a system with procedures, protocols, and controls? In the end, the state overturned 21,587 drug convictions due to Dookhan's misconduct.[9]

By automatically accepting any result from an accredited lab, there is an increased risk that problems will be missed or ignored due to cognitive bias about their reliability. If the defence expert doesn't have accreditation (and many don't, especially if they are small companies or sole providers), the court's attitude may simply hinge on who is accredited and who is not, and ignore defence experts' cries of exasperation. That's how we end up with what happened with the Birmingham Six, which is discussed a little later in this section.

---

[8]   K. Mettler, 'How a Lab Chemist Went from 'Superwoman' to Disgraced Saboteur of More than 20,000 Drug Cases', *Washington Post* (21 April 2017). Available at https://www.washingtonpost.com/news/morning-mix/wp/2017/04/21/how-a-lab-chemist-went-from-superwoman-to-disgraced-saboteur-of-more-than-20000-drug-cases/.

[9]   J. Donahue and E. Gully-Santiago, *Supreme Judicial Court Dismisses Over 21,000 Cases Affected by the Breach at the Hinton State Laboratory Institute*, Supreme Judicial Court of Massachusetts Press Release (20 April 2017). Available at https://www.mass.gov/news/supreme-judicial-court-dismisses-over-21000-cases-affected-by-the-breach-at-the-hinton-state-laboratory-institute.

The problems with accreditation and its reliability are complicated by the fact that it is *methods* that are accredited, not people or labs. It is possible to have a lab that has many accredited methods, but happens to use one that is not and neglects to disclose this fact.

In one case, the defendant, Mr. A, was charged with—of all things—breaching a Tree Preservation Order (TPO) by allegedly poisoning three oak trees in his garden with glyphosate. By way of background, a small group of houses had been built on the edge of a protected forest in a countryside setting of idyllic tranquillity. Each house sat on a generous lot with ample garden space before the treeline.

In the garden, over 30 metres from Mr. A's house, were three oak trees. One day, these were found to be rapidly dying. Drill holes were found around the base of each tree, and it looked like someone had poisoned them.

All eyes turned to Mr. A, who owned and lived in the house. The alleged motive was to create more light and space in his garden.

This might seem plausible in the abstract, but you need to appreciate that close behind the trees was the forest. It didn't make sense to get rid of just those three trees, as it made no difference to either the space in the garden or the amount of light. But the trees *did* block light to a neighbour's house—one who had been found cutting limbs from Mr. A's trees without asking his permission a month earlier.

Breaching a TPO is a magistrate's matter and carries only a nominal fine, but Mr. A was adamant he was innocent and questioned the forensic work that had been done to show the trees had been poisoned by glyphosate. He asked that the case be heard in Crown Court.

The forensic work had been done by an accredited lab, and the lab certificates said, "These laboratory certificates have been produced in accordance with an ISO accredited method." The trouble was that this was entirely literal: the method used in the case had *not* been validated for samples taken from trees, nor was it accredited. It was the *layout* of the certificate—i.e. the words it contained and how the text had been presented on the digital document titled "Certificate of Analysis"—that had been produced in accordance with an accredited method. When you read down the certificate, there was a test code and a letter "N" next to it, which led to an index on another page defining this as a "non-accredited method." It took an expert to spot this, as nobody else had. There had been an assumption that the analysis was fully supported by accreditation and was therefore accurate.

But even after the defence pointed this out to the lab and the certificates had been reissued, the lab continued to do the same thing. UKAS had signed off on this approach, and it was the only way they were permitted to report their results. Naturally, the lab didn't want to mislead anyone on purpose, but it also shows that people won't read the small print *and* will make assumptions about the evidence based on—in this case—expectation bias.

In addition to the fact the method was not accredited, I found obvious discrepancies in the data when I reviewed it. It turned out all three results had been reported incorrectly. The lab diligently corrected the results, at which point nothing made any sense: three different samples were taken from two different trees alleged to have been poisoned at the same time, but there were three completely different results. No-one could figure out why.

Part of the problem was a lack of understanding of what a lab should look for, how long the poison might last, and whether it could be found in the samples after a certain length of time. Even before the lab received the samples for testing, there had been concerns about how the samples were taken and the possibility of contamination or cross-contamination. The fact the method was not accredited and therefore not validated was a massive issue in the case. Mr. A was eventually found not guilty, having spent what I can only assume was a small fortune on legal fees by then.

When dealing with cognitive bias (and arguably some actual bias), one of the most infamous forensic cases that crops up concerns the use of the Griess test and expert evidence, as detailed in the judge's summary in *R v. McIlkenny, Hunter, Walker, Callaghan, Hill and Power*, also known as the Birmingham Six.

Six Irishmen were arrested a few days following the November 1974 bombing of two bars in Birmingham in which 21 people were killed.[10] Their hands were swabbed to test for nitrites using the Griess test and subsequent analysis was conducted as needed. Even in the 1970s, it was recognised that the test for nitrites was not specific to explosives: although finding nitrites on someone's hands might suggest they had handled nitroglycerine-based explosives, this was not necessarily conclusive.

Of the six Irishmen arrested, two were found to have a positive nitrite test on their hands. Dr. Skuse, the prosecution expert, stated in court that he was 99% certain some of the men had recently handled high explosives. The defence expert, Dr. Black, told the court (correctly) that the test was not specific to nitroglycerine, but it was not until 1991 that research showed the same result could be obtained from handling things like playing cards.

You might think that in the presence of any doubt, there could be no question as to what the jury should do: they would surely have to consider the test not to be non-specific to nitroglycerine. But how could they form an independent view when told the following by a judge:

> "Of course, if in forming your own judgment on this matter you prefer Dr. Black's view to Dr. Skuse's view, then you will obviously conclude that the forensic evidence of Dr. Skuse is of no value. Indeed Dr. Black's theory logically seems to imply not only that Dr. Skuse's theories were of no value, but that Dr. Skuse has been spending and must have spent much of his

---

[10] B. Knight, 'Forensic Chemistry in the Dock', *New Scientist* 1986 (14 July 1995). Available at https://www.newscientist.com/article/mg14719864-300-forensic-chemistry-in-the-dock/.

professional life wasting his time because, if Dr. Black is right, the Griess test was not worth carrying out … Do you think that Dr. Skuse has been wasting most of his professional time? It is a matter entirely for you."[11]

Imagine what the judge might have said if the laboratory method used by Dr. Skuse had also been accredited. (Although, had this been the case, they would arguably have done a proper validation study in the first place, and probably found substances which can produce false positives—even if they didn't think to test playing cards.[12])

As it currently stands, in criminal forensics, most laboratory work done for the prosecution is done using a lab with accredited methods. Most defence expert work is not. It's only a matter of time before the prosecution will seek to bar a defence expert for failing to use accredited methods.

As touched on earlier, part of the problem in all of this is the language around accreditation. People are not accredited. Methods and procedures are accredited. Laboratories are only accredited when they are using methods which have been accredited.

However, to the lay person (and in some cases, to experts—as demonstrated in a recent trial where an expert replied, "Yes" when if asked if he was accredited), there is no such distinction. Clients will assume that if a lab is 'accredited' then everything they do must be accredited; lay persons will think that it is the expert who is accredited, rather than the method they have used. They won't necessarily know that opinions given by experts are not accredited.

---

[11] *R v. McIlkenny and Others* (1991) EWCA Crim 2. Available at https://www.bailii.org/ew/cases/EWCA/Crim/1991/2.html.

[12] Validation studies are performed to check if a method is reliable. A validation study should highlight the consistency and accuracy of a method by testing known items, but also—critically—where its limitations lie. In this case, an obvious part of a validation study would be to see what other chemicals might trigger a false positive when using the Griess test.

This said, most accredited organisations will undertake a portion of work that uses non-accredited methods. Forensics is about human nature, and in human nature something that needs analysis, but is too uncommon, impractical, or implausible to create and maintain an accreditation for, will always come up.

For example, a drug analysis lab will have accredited methods for analysing cannabis, cocaine, amphetamine, methamphetamine, diazepam, heroin, MDMA (3,4-methylenedioxymethamphetamine ecstasy) and so on. Each of these must be accredited on their own. But if the lab receives a white powder that doesn't appear to exist in the normal libraries but is suspected to be used in creating amphetamine, they may analyse the powder with a method that is not accredited. The justice system cannot afford to wait for up to a year for a full research project to be done just so that accredited can be awarded for a single case, and so the lab will report that their analysis has relied on a method outside of the scope of accreditation.

ISO 17025 and 17020 are international standards. In theory, asking for an assessment provider from the EU or US would help create a competitive environment and keep costs low, but this is not allowed. In the UK, UKAS is the sole body recognised by the government, giving them a monopoly.

Moreover, accreditation is done on a per-method basis, so if your lab has 20 different drug analysis methods, that's 20 difference accreditations, each with their own price tag to create and then maintain through annual inspections.

Defence experts often work for small companies which can't afford the initial and recurring costs of accreditation. If the court bars them from giving evidence because they are not accredited, they will go out of business. And if that happens, who will be the check on prosecution experts?

Unless funding or some other alternative is proposed for smaller providers, then the push to 'improve quality' will effectively bar defence teams from getting suitable experts (accredited or not) to check their work and ultimately reduce checks and balances in the criminal justice system. (You might wonder if this point should be raised with the government, and it has: I've told the House of Lords so myself.[13])

Another important form of bias not discussed in the FSR guidance is *status quo bias*.

The expression 'You can't teach an old dog new tricks' (or, in its literal form relating to sheep dogs, an "olde dogge to stoupe")[14] is one of several which convey the difficulty of encouraging people set in their ways to take on new things. Subconsciously, people will disproportionately stick with the status quo rather than risk trying something else.[15]

As an example, let's consider the field of fingerprint comparisons, where doctrinal practice has remained in place for over a hundred years with relatively little core theoretical change.

The current fingerprint comparison model has three outcomes: identification, inconclusive, and exclude. Almost every other forensic discipline uses a statistical or stated level of support (e.g. '1 in n'), or varying degrees of probability (e.g. 'moderate support'). Very few produce a clearly stated "identification."

Using handwriting comparison—another very old forensic method—as an example, it can be common for one expert to say there was 'extremely strong support' for Ms. S being the author of a sample, and another expert to say they thought it was 'strong support'. These are two different opinions, but at least they are in the same ballpark. In fingerprints, this isn't an option.

---

[13] House of Lords Science and Technology Select Committee, *Forensic Science and the Criminal Justice System: A Blueprint for Change*, HL Paper 333, UK Parliament (1 May 2019). Available at https://publications.parliament.uk/pa/ld201719/ldselect/ldsctech/333/33302.htm. I was one of the witnesses called to give evidence to the inquiry.

[14] See A. Fitzherbert, *Fitzherbert's Book of Husbandry* (Stephen Austin and Sons, 1882 [1534]).

[15] W. Samuelson and R. Zeckhauser, 'Status Quo Bias in Decision Making', *Journal of Risk and Uncertainty* 1 7–59 (1988). Available at https://doi.org/10.1007/BF00055564.

Two experts might, in their hearts, think the probability is 'extremely strong support', but that category doesn't exist in fingerprint comparison. Depending on the individual, one expert might end up calling it an "identification" and the other, "inconclusive." While they might have the same underlying view of the evidence, the restrictions imposed on them by the (accredited) process makes it look like they have very different opinions.

This problem is particularly seen in cases where marks are poor. The fingerprint expert is forced into a narrow decision-making process: whether to call something an "identification" or "exclusion" (knowing they risk getting shot down if this turns out to be incorrect), or to call it "inconclusive" (and risk the prosecution dropping the case for lack of evidence). If the case in question concerns a horrific crime, and the suspect stands to walk free as a result of this decision, then the fingerprint expert has an extremely difficult decision to make.

Arguably, it would be better to adopt a scale of support, but this has not happened in over 100 years of fingerprint comparison. Status quo bias will say that there's nothing wrong with the current approach despite headline news of false positive cases, validation studies, proficiency test studies, and research to the contrary, including recent articles.[16]

Although the FSR is responsible for quality assurance in UK forensics, its guidelines for dealing with fingerprint comparison supported the same questionable dogma that has been in existence for over a century until just recently. In 2020, the FSR appendix for fingerprints was amended to state that the term "Identified" "…will be replaced in the future when an evaluative interpretation method for fingerprint comparison is further developed,"[17] offering the possibility of change.

---

[16] See, for example, R.A. Hicklin et al., 'Why Do Latent Fingerprint Examiners Differ in Their Conclusions?', *Forensic Sci. Intl.* 316 110542 (2020). Available at https://doi.org/10.1016/j.forsciint.2020.110542.

[17] Forensic Science Regulator, *Codes of Practice and Conduct: Friction Ridge Detail (Fingerprint Comparison) FSR-C-128.* (2020). Available at https://assets.publishing.service.gov.uk/government/uploads/system/uploads/attachment_data/file/914695/FSR-C-128__Issue3.pdf.

This brings about another consideration. If the current method *will* change, then, by inference, the FSR has acknowledged that the current method isn't good enough. However, the document does not state this, and no timeframe for introducing the change or replacement scale is provided. In the meantime, UKAS will be accrediting fingerprint departments in accordance with a doctrine with an expiry date on it. The doorway to change has been opened, but when or how the old dogge will learn to stoupe remains to be seen.

The shortlist of subconscious preferences (cognitive biases) included in the full FSR guidance, along with the definitions provided, includes:

- **A. *Expectation bias,*** also known as experimenter's bias, where the expectation of what an individual will find affects what is actually found.

This is the 'cart before the horse' problem in science.

A famous example, published by R. Anderson in the *Journal of Forensic Sciences,*[18] concerns the notion that if beads of copper in wires are formed before a fire starts (i.e. if they cause the fire), they would show a different (cleaner) composition compared with wire that is exposed to a fire and then short-circuits after the insulation burns away, as the molten copper would have absorbed smoke and other gases.

It's a valid theory, and in fire investigation, whether an electrical 'bead' caused or was caused by a fire is an age-old question. If it was possible to determine this by analysis, such a method would be worth millions to the insurance industry, not to mention being a critical test for suspected arson cases. According to Anderson, "If the electrical short circuit occurred before the fire had started, then arc bead analysis would show the absence of combustion products."[19]

---

[18] R.N. Anderson, 'Surface Analysis of Electrical Arc Residues in Fire Investigation', *Journal of Forensic Sciences* 34(3) 633–637 (1989).

[19] Ibid.

Bear in mind that this was a peer-reviewed paper in a distinguished forensic journal; it was incredible news which took the fire investigation community by (electric) storm. The only catch is that Anderson's theory wasn't true. Molten copper doesn't work that way, as another article in the *Journal* would go on to explain.[20]

Anderson was arguably expecting to find a result to support his theory. It's a common thread in research—and in a way, why bother to research something unless you think you are going to get some kind of useful outcome? After all, there is a lot of pressure for funding research in order to get *results*.

This sort of error crops up from time to time in any process, including those in accredited forensic laboratories.

In one case, Simon was accused of being a heroin dealer. Two small plastic bags were recovered during a search of his house. One contained a small amount of brown powder, which he accepted was heroin for personal use, and the other about 30 grams of fine white powder. Simon was adamant it was glucose.

The samples were sent to an accredited forensic lab and both items came back as heroin. As far as the police were concerned, Simon was lying. But think about it: one powder was brown, and the other was fine and white in colour. Those who work with drug cases, including the scientist who did the analysis, the scientist who peer-reviewed the report, and the police officer in charge of the case, should know that heroin has not been encountered as a fine white powder in the UK since the 1970s, when it redirected pharmacy stock.

Even without having to do any additional work, the description of each item alone should have made it apparent that there was an issue.

---

[20] D. Howitt, 'The Surface Analysis of Copper Arc Beads—A Critical Review', *Journal of Forensic Sciences* 42(4) 608–609 (1997).

At this point, you would hope that the police had a conversation with the forensic lab to address this, but they didn't. Could this have been because it might have cost the police money? Or was it because of the expectation bias that defendants lie and accredited forensic labs get it right because, well, they're accredited?

When samples of suspected drugs are analysed, they are often put in tiny glass vials onto a rack, which then goes into an 'auto-sampler'. Each position on the rack has a number, which is entered into the auto-sampler sequence log to tell it which vial to select and which exhibit it has come from. In Simon's case, what happened was that the analyst had programmed to run the brown powder (which I'll call 'Simon1') at position 32, then, on the next line, to run the white powder 'Simon2' at position 33—but they accidentally typed this as 32 in the sampler sequence. It ran the brown heroin powder twice, but labelled as two different exhibits.

Sequence logs are normally checked for errors like this, and there was indeed a quality check (QC) signature on the form, despite the QC checker having missed that '32' appeared twice. The checker had likely expected the log to be correct (because it usually is) and therefore overlooked the error. Despite the police and the lab having an opportunity to catch the mistake, it was the defence expert that pointed this out and did the analysis. The white powder was, as Simon said, glucose.

- **B. *Confirmation bias*** is closely related to expectation bias, whereby people test hypotheses by looking for confirmatory evidence rather than potentially contradictory evidence.

In a way, we are all very familiar with this. Just have a conversation on any subject (drugs, religion, or the coronavirus) with someone who truly believes what they say despite overt evidence to the contrary.

For example, I have no strong opinions on the legalisation of cannabis. I have seen its medical benefits as well as its unwanted effects, but what I don't understand are those who claim that smoking cannabis can cure cancer. The smoke portfolio from cannabis contains thousands of chemicals, and there are bound to be a dozen or more in the mix which are known to cause cancer. Not because it's cannabis, but because that's just what you get when you burn *any* plant.

I understand this because I'm a chemist, but believers (who aren't) don't want to hear this, and—usually after a long and painful conversation—I'm told that I'm just "anti-drug."

As we've discussed, it's very hard to dissuade someone set in their ways, and the same is true of those who give expert evidence. Once people have made up their minds about something, they will often ignore the bits of the puzzle that no longer fit.

Rooted in this is the concept of open-minded thinking. In *Thinking and Deciding*,[21] psychology professor Jonathan Baron discusses actively open-minded thinking, as well as three things that can go wrong with 'search-inference' thinking:

1. Our search misses something that it should have uncovered, or we act with a high degree of confidence despite little effort.

2. We seek evidence and inferences in ways that prevent us from choosing the best possibility (tunnel vision).

3. We think too much.

I'm in the third camp, but I would also argue that in order to think open-mindedly, we have to approach an issue from many angles. The question is: at what point does it become too much?

The second category is where the problem is most serious: a person who makes decisions based on evidence that favours their preferred outcome, which can lead to over-confidence in their decision.

---

[21] J. Baron, *Thinking and Deciding*, 3rd edn. (Cambridge University Press, 2000).

Earlier on, we talked about how fingerprint experts have often made bold and sweeping statements. Take the case of Harry Jackson, who was accused of stealing billiard balls. According to the case transcripts from 1902,[22] the expert in the case stated, "I have no doubt whatever that the impression on the window sash and those taken by Collins of the prisoner's hand at Brixton Prison, are identical."

Given landmark Court of Appeal cases which have highlighted the existence of false positives, you would think that, after 115 years, the UK would have conducted extensive research into determining the frequency with which false positives are identified. They have not, and statements of absolute certainty such as, "I have no doubt whatsoever" persist. What we *do* have is a confirmation bias loop that is very hard to break.

Thankfully, our friends in the US aren't as shy. The Federal Bureau of Investigation (FBI) published a study on fingerprint false positive rates,[23] which, along with other unpublished studies, went into the 2016 President's Council of Advisors on Science and Technology (PCAST) report to President Obama.[24]

The FBI got 169 fingerprint experts to each compare 100 pairs of latent and reference prints from a pool of 744 pairs. These, in turn, had been drawn from comparable fingerprints taken from the Automated Fingerprint Identification System (AFIS) database of 58 million subjects. They found that five examiners made false positive errors (0.1%), and 85% made at least 1 false negative. The false positives and most of the

---

[22] Trial of Harry Jackson, Old Bailey Proceedings Online (www.oldbaileyonline.org, version 8.0, 14 January 2022), t19020909-686 (September 1902). Trial text available at https://www.oldbaileyonline.org/browse.jsp?id=t19020909-686&div=t19020909-686&terms=jackson#highlight.

[23] B.T. Ulery et al., 'Accuracy and Reliability of Forensic Latent Fingerprint Decisions', *Proceedings of the National Academy of Sciences* 108(19) 7733–7738 (2011). Available at https://doi.org/10.1073/pnas.1018707108.

[24] President's Council of Advisors on Science and Technology, *Report to the President, Forensic Science in Criminal Courts: Ensuring Scientific Validity of Feature-Comparison Methods* (September 2016). Available at https://obamawhitehouse.archives.gov/sites/default/files/microsites/ostp/PCAST/pcast_forensic_science_report_final.pdf.

false negatives were caught in the second round of checks, so no false positives made it into the final reporting. It was noted that the experts frequently differed on whether the fingerprints were suitable for comparison.

The PCAST report used other unpublished studies, such a 2014 one from Miami-Dade which was commissioned by the US Department of Justice (but not published by them).[25] The Miami-Dade report examiners had a false positive rate of 3% and a false negative rate of 7.5%. These values dropped to 0% for false positives and 2.9% for false negatives at the second round of checks (the verification stage).

The idea that the verification check resolved the false positive rate to zero might be of some comfort, but when you bear in mind the sheer volume of fingerprint comparisons which are done, the risk of an initial false positive being missed on verification is all too real.

In the last chapter, I mentioned that eyewitness evidence risks critical failure when uncertainty, bias, and confidence are present. Applying the same concept to fingerprints, uncertainty at the initial verification stages should be expressed as part of the fingerprint package, but it isn't. Even in cases where there is uncertainty at the outset, if the process ends with an identification, this will be stated with absolute certainty when it reaches the witness box.

Fingerprint comparison is not the only area where expressions of certainty are used. Another is the world of forensic firearms and toolmark comparisons.

When a gun is fired, the cartridge can end up with distinct marks embedded on its casing, caused by the pressure of the discharge against metal surfaces. This includes the breech, firing pin, and ejector mark (if there is one). The pattern and location of these marks is treated in much the

---

[25] I. Pacheco, B. Cerchiai, and S. Stoiloff, *Miami-Dade Research Study for the Reliability of the ACE-V Process: Accuracy and Precision in Latent Fingerprint Examinations*, US Department of Justice (December 2014). Available at https://www.ojp.gov/pdffiles1/nij/grants/248534.pdf.

same way as fingerprints in that no two guns are the same. At a microscopic level, I would agree, but much like fingerprints, examiners are not looking at the machined faces themselves. Rather, what they study are the actual marks left on cartridges from a scene, as compared to test-fired cartridges from a weapon that was seized in relation to the incident.

Most of the validation and competency work revolves around setting tasks for the expert to determine which gun the suspect-fired cartridge had come from, where one of the casings in question came from a gun which was test-fired. In such scenarios, the examiner's results are exceptionally good.

But what about a potential real-world scenario where, let's say, a gun was seized in the belief that it had fired the cartridges, but it hadn't? How good are the analysts at excluding the firearm? Has anyone studied this?

Again, we turn to PCAST, who reported that where reference samples from the gun that fired the questioned cartridge were present in the study, false positive rates were very low (0.02%). However, when studies were done where, unbeknownst to the examiner, some of the questioned cartridges came from a gun where no reference samples had been provided, the false positive rate jumped to 1.5–2%. That's a 200-fold increase.

When it comes to open-minded thinking, if your initial assessment is a false positive, how much more would you do to then prove the opposite (i.e. that you are wrong)? Unlike DNA, which mitigates the chance of a false positive by using statistics, the danger—particularly with fingerprint or firearm evidence—is that the lack of an open-minded approach, coupled with overstating the strength of evidence, means in cases of false positives, there is the risk of an innocent person going to jail. This might be for no other reason than that any inconsistencies contradicting the fingerprint match might be disregarded, as the fingerprint evidence will be firmly anchored (see below), and, is, therefore, assumed to be correct.

This structure forces a situation where uncertainty plus confirmation bias leads to confidence. What might have started out ambiguous ends up being labelled as "identified."

This is one reason why contextual bias can play a very negative role in the examiner's ability to be objective in the early stages of assessment. This said, in other cases, the forensic report becomes meaningless without additional context.

- **C. *Anchoring effects or focalism*** are closely related to both of the above (expectation and confirmation bias) and occur when an individual relies too heavily on an initial piece of information when making subsequent judgements, which are then interpreted on the basis of the anchor.

Have you ever asked someone for a cup of coffee and been given tea instead by mistake? I have, and when I spat the coffee back into the mug and said, "You sure this coffee's okay?," the person replied, "Oh, I'm so sorry, I made tea by mistake." And suddenly, it tasted just fine. In my head I was drinking the worst coffee in the world, but once the anchoring information changed, it was a fine cup of tea.

In a popular northern city is a pub that sits close to a towpath, next to a slow-moving river. The pub has a doorway which opens straight onto the path. When you enter, there's a bar to the right which opens into a sitting area with chairs and tables. At the opposite side of the room is a doorway leading to the men's room.

On a warm and sunny weekend afternoon, a man in his late teens walked into a pub and asked to use the toilet. The barman, who was standing behind the bar at that point, agreed. The toilet block was a small affair, with a short one-metre square entrance and a second door into a two by three metre room with two urinals and one toilet cubicle. The teen was in there for a few minutes. As he left, he walked right under a CCTV camera hanging over the doorway.

A minute later, a man in his forties, one of the regulars at the bar, went to use the toilet. He came back out, calmly walked to the bar, and told the bar staff that there was a fire inside the toilet. The barman went to get a bucket of water (leaving aside the question of why there wasn't a fire extinguisher to hand), and made several unsuccessful attempts to extinguish the fire. In the end, the Fire Service arrived reasonably quickly and put it out.

The young man was soon identified from the CCTV, arrested, and charged with arson with intent to endanger life and arson reckless as to whether life was endangered. He had no previous criminal history, had done well at school, and was looking at university places. When interviewed by the police, he said he had been walking with his friends by the river and needed to use the toilet. That was it. The case went to trial.

The investigating officer fully believed the young man did it, but I wonder how much of his assumption was anchored on the fact that a) he was a teenager (and therefore up to no good); and b) he had been the last person seen on camera leaving the toilets. If not him, who else could have done it? I would argue that if the suspect had been a decorated WW2 veteran, the investigation would have been very different. Unfortunately for him, he was a young man.

The logic behind all this is flawed. The last person to enter the toilet wasn't actually the teenager: it was the man, the bar regular, who discovered and reported the fire. Despite this, the case papers didn't mention him: not even his name or what he saw when he went inside the toilet. He wasn't even interviewed.

The CCTV recording wasn't served in full and only the clip showing the teenager going in and leaving was provided. When the full footage was requested, the barman—who had said in a written statement that he feared for the life of his customers—was shown calmly clearing tables while waiting for the fire brigade to arrive. There was no apparent evacuation of the premises.

One has to wonder why he mentioned fearing for his customers' lives in his statement. Could it have been suggested to him that this would support a charge of endangerment to life? Did he genuinely feel this, or did he feel compelled to say it? Whatever the reason, the actions captured in the CCTV footage were not those of someone fearing for his own safety or anyone else's.

Because the investigation was intent on finding the young man guilty, they never bothered to interview the man who discovered the fire, even as the young man maintained his innocence. A truly open-minded thought process would have insisted on scrutinising the investigation, but cognitive bias precluded that. Investigators put all their resources into trying to show what they already *thought* was the truth, regardless of what the defendant had said (confirmation bias). Why? Was it because of the anchoring effect from the start, caused by the CCTV showing the teenager?

The full CCTV footage showed that the regular who discovered and reported the fire spent 20 seconds inside the toilet. Given how small the toilet was, and that it was allegedly on fire when he went in, why was he in there for so long?

When investigating a fire, you always try to interview the person who discovered it. One reason for doing this is that, in a small number of cases, they are the person who started it. This is known as the 'hero effect'—basically an attention-seeking act.

Twenty seconds was long enough for the man to have started a fire. Even though this critical point was raised by the defence expert, *the case still went to trial.*

Counsel for the defence raised the point with the prosecutor before the trial started, and the prosecutor asked the officer-in-charge to find the man who had discovered the fire and call him as a witness. The man was a regular at the pub, so the police asked the bartender if he knew who he was. The bartender replied that the man hadn't been to the pub since the incident.

The Crown offered no evidence, and the young man, whose parents and younger sister had shown up to support him, was in shock. He had cancelled his college plans and, for nine months, wondered how he was going to go against the might of what seemed to be a damning investigation with 'proof' that he was the offender. Had a defence expert not been involved, he might have gone to jail.

The whole case suffered from an early anchoring effect caused by the belief that the "last person" in the toilets was the perpetrator, when the CCTV footage showed this was actually the bar regular who reported the fire. Despite the obvious holes in the case identified before trial, no one could be dissuaded from this.

When leaving the courthouse, I came across the investigating officer, who was red-faced and understandably angry. He stopped me and said, "We'll get him next time, maybe when he kills someone."

It bothered me that he seemed to think this was somehow my fault, but then I had to remind myself that to some people, I am squarely on the dark side.

"I think you've missed the point," I told him. "You've just spent nine months chasing a teenager when the real arsonist is still walking around your city."

- **D. *Contextual bias*** is when someone has other information aside from that being considered, which influences (either consciously or subconsciously) the outcome of the consideration.

The biggest problem in forensic science is context, because forensics is a context-based science. Our techniques are often designed for other applications, only for someone to have an epiphany and realise they might also work for criminal investigations. Presumptive blood tests used at crime scenes were originally developed for looking at blood in stool samples. Prostate specific antigen (PSA) tests for semen in sexual assault cases were born out of a test for prostate problems. Cell site analysis is a by-product of how phone networks collect data for billing purposes.

When these tests are used in a sanitised environment, the results and their interpretation are linear. If you're looking at a stool sample and you get a positive for blood, then it's almost certainly blood. If you do the same test in forensics, then you are applying a relatively easy and unsophisticated test in a massively complex environment. If you get a positive result, what does this mean? Is it human blood or hamburger dripping? Could it be rust, broccoli, bleach, and so on?

What makes forensic science different from 'normal' science is that we are constantly using well-defined tests and procedures which generate specific results, but trying to understand what those results mean in the context of a hugely uncontrolled environment. A change in context can completely change what a result means.

We have talked a lot about fingerprint comparison and the idea of separating the actual fingerprint analysis from any context, so as to ensure no undue pressure is placed on the expert in forming their opinion. This seems fair in the abstract, but context must be considered at some point, and the expert needs to be made aware of this to ensure it has no bearing on any opinions they have formed or may be asked about in court.

Context, such as *how* a fingerprint got to be there, is critical to understanding its relevance in a case. The current push is to reduce exposure to contextual information so as not to subconsciously prejudice an expert. So whose job is it to look at the context and see if it makes sense?

The fingerprint expert might see their role as fairly isolated: they have made an identification, but what it means in the context of the case isn't their problem. The court may see contextual interpretation as the role of the jury, but this assumes that any issues *have* actually come to light for the jury to consider. The officer-in-charge may think they can make that determination as they understand the wider context of the case. The barristers may feel they can weed out the interpretation as they've seen it before.

But who is qualified to understand and decide on technical issues of context, such as the longevity or orientation of fingerprints? It has to be an expert.

By way of an example: after a burglary at a clubhouse, a crime scene investigator (CSI) took fingerprint lifts from the cellar door, which had been forced open. The fingerprint was matched to a person who had a previous conviction for burglary. (This is basically the summary of the factual evidence.)

The suspect said he had been to the clubhouse, but this was four years earlier. The clubhouse owner stated that the door in question had been painted 18 months before, so the Crown argued that the suspect must have been lying as the fingerprint could not survive being painted over. (This is the context.)

It looked like an open-and-shut case (no pun intended), but the suspect was adamant that it wasn't him, so the matter was handed to a defence expert to examine the fingerprint lifts and photographs. These plainly showed the paint that had been lifted around the fingerprint—and revealed the same fingerprint on the paint below. In other words, the suspect's fingerprint had been in the original layer of paint, and the paint used to decorate the door was so thin that the mark had come right through. The CSI had lifted a mark that was four years old.

You might have hoped that a well-trained CSI would have spotted this, but they didn't. The fingerprint expert should have spotted this, but they had only worked with a photograph of the mark and didn't. Despite the signs that the mark was four years old, the idea that any painting over would have obliterated the mark came to anchor the case—without any testing to support it. Neither the fingerprint expert nor the CSI were told of the context, which would have prompted them to go back and check things over. Paradoxically, the *lack* of context created the bias that almost sent an innocent person to jail.

In another similar case, a fingerprint mark was found on a railing in a position that would have been physically impossible to achieve in the context of a burglary. It was, however, perfectly easy to explain that it had been deposited in the paint coating on the railing by the lad who had delivered it—and, as it turned out, also worked for the company that made the railing many years previously.

There was another case with a fingerprint in glue on a drainpipe which had been there since the pipe was installed. There was one on a plastic bag which turned out to be outside the property and was probably just garbage. A mark was on a frame of a window that a young lad had helped manufacture over a decade before.

The fingerprints in all of these cases correctly identified the person arrested, but it took a defence expert to figure out what had happened. Without that, the evidence would have favoured the prosecution.

One of the most notorious examples of context bias involves fingerprint evidence in the 2004 Madrid bombing.[26]

On 11 March 2004, bombs were detonated on several Madrid commuter trains, killing around 200 people. The Spanish National Police (SNP) recovered a bag containing detonators which were linked to the attack and sent them to Interpol, with a request that the FBI assist in finding fingerprints.

On 19 March 2004, the FBI identified a fingerprint as belonging to Brandon Mayfield. This was based on a search using an automated system known as the Integrated Automated Fingerprint Identification System (IAFIS), which was checked and verified by an examiner, checked by a second examiner, and then once more by a unit chief.

In forensics, million-to-one coincidences seem to happen a lot, and this case is no different. Mayfield was an Oregon-based lawyer who had

---

[26] Office of the Inspector General (Oversight and Review Division), *A Review of the FBI's Handling of the Brandon Mayfield Case*, US Department of Justice (March 2006). Available at https://oig.justice.gov/sites/default/files/archive/special/s0601/Chapter1.pdf.

represented a convicted terrorist in a child custody dispute, and who had had contact with suspected terrorists. However, there were no links between him and the Madrid bombings.

On 13 April 2004, the FBI found that the SNP's own fingerprint exam had discounted the fingerprint as belonging to Mayfield. This should have prompted an internal review at the FBI, but—perhaps due to anchoring bias—they instead sent an FBI examiner to Spain to explain their rationale to the SNP, who in turn said that they would review it.

Mayfield was arrested on 6 May 2004 and his house and office searched. He denied that it was his fingerprint on the bag, but he was placed in remand in Portland, Oregon. The court ordered an independent review of the fingerprint evidence and on 19 May 2004, an independent examiner submitted a report agreeing with the FBI's findings. That same day, the SNP said they had identified the fingerprint to an Algerian named Ouhnane Daoud.

After reviewing the evidence, on 24 May 2004, the FBI withdrew its identification of Mayfield. Reasons given for the misidentification included the high-pressure nature of the case, overconfidence in IAFIS, and cognitive bias on the part of the reviewers, as they had known the result of the original examination.

An investigation and report by the Office of the Inspector General found several factors that led to the misidentification. The first was the similarity of the fingerprints.

Now, in a way, this is a given. I would argue that had the fingerprint *not* been similar it would never have been selected by either IAFIS or included by the first examiner. In other words, issues of false positives only occur in cases where the fingerprints are similar and the larger the databases searched, the greater the chance a very similar fingerprint will appear.

A false positive fingerprint has to be one of the most dangerous and damning pieces of evidence. Since they will almost always occur in similar fingerprints, all procedures and methods must revolve around understanding when a fingerprint appears to be a *match* versus when it happens to be only *similar*. (DNA analysis suffers from the same risk, but this is dealt with in a very different way; a number is assigned to the level of confidence in the result.)

If we follow the cognitive bias model, the problem arguably started when IAFIS created an expectation bias when it found at least one potential fingerprint match.

Another issue raised involved expectation bias. The process should first start by assessing the questioned, poorer-quality mark and identifying any features that can be considered reliable for a comparison, and *then* comparing it to the high-quality reference. In this case, the examiner looked at Mayfield's reference fingerprint and compared it to the questioned mark, which created a risk of 'seeing' additional points of match because they were expected to be there.

The report lists several other reasons, one of which you might have thought of already: when, on 13 April 2004, the SNP said that the print wasn't a match for Mayfield, why did the FBI try to convince the SNP of the rightness of their explanation (and therefore, by extension, that the SNP must be wrong), as opposed to going back to the start and checking everything all over again? This is the same problem we often see when working for the defence: if you disagree with the Crown's expert, a common reaction is to argue that we (i.e. the defence expert) must be wrong, followed by the Crown's expert creating reasons why this is the case. In other words: confirmation bias.

What the report did find was that being a high-profile terrorist case was *not* a factor. You might be surprised by this, but then—as the report goes on to say—the FBI is routinely involved in all sorts of high-profile cases, including terrorism, without making errors.

The FBI did apologise to Mayfield for its mistake, but that's not where this story ends.[27] This section is about contextual bias, and here is what happened afterwards.

A subsequent study took five fingerprint experts from the UK, US, Israel, the Netherlands and Australia, with a mean level of 17 years of experience.[28] The experts, who were not familiar with Mayfield's fingerprint, were asked to review the FBI's erroneous match between a fingerprint from the scene and Mayfield's, but were told to ignore this and form their own assessment.

Each expert was actually given one of their own previous cases from 2000, which they had previously determined was a match. Despite being given one of their own past cases, only one of the five correctly stated the fingerprint evidence was a match. The other four changed their opinion: one said there was insufficient evidence, and three contradicted their previous report.

It was *that* easy to change the context and change the result. And this is just fingerprints.

The idea of reducing context as much as possible to avoid contextual bias can actually lead to huge issues of bias when forensic findings are interpreted by people who are not experts in that area, such as the officer-in-charge, detective or the prosecutor. Is it better for an expert to be made aware of the context—along with how to mitigate against bias and construct hypotheses about scenarios they are informed of (provided it is also understood that the context being given may itself be biased)—or to not involve the expert and leave things to chance?

---

[27] FBI Press Release, *Statement on the Brandon Mayfield Case*, FBI National Press Office (24 May 2004). Available at https://archives.fbi.gov/archives/news/pressrel/press-releases/statement-on-brandon-mayfield-case.

[28] I.E. Dror, D. Charlton, and A. Peron, 'Contextual Information Renders Experts Vulnerable to Making Erroneous Identifications', *Forensic Science International* 156 74–78 (2006). Available at https://doi.org/10.1016/j.forsciint.2005.10.017.

One solution proposed by Dror is Linear Sequential Unmasking (LSU),[29] which would allow examiners to report their findings without any context at all, followed by reference samples, and then, as late as possible, the context relevant material. This would shield examiners from the effects of bias.

The LSU model should work, but the current forensic model doesn't allow for it in terms of economics or logistics. When faced with 12 boxes of, say, clothing evidence to examine in a triple murder, if there is no context at all, then all the items are given equal weight. It would take weeks or months to examine them when only a few might be of critical relevance, and in that time the evidential trail could go well and truly cold. There must be some dialogue to direct the analysis, which means some context *has* to be given.

If steps are taken to mitigate any contextual bias at that stage, the LSU model could be a way to proceed, but the economics then become an issue. Doing an initial analysis, followed by more work as the context is unmasked, means more resources. If the lab doing the work is privatised, such as in England and Wales, then there will also be additional costs. Those submitting evidence to private labs (such as a scientific support manager (SSM) already choose which items are sent away for analysis and those which are not, with one reason being to save money. The SSM, in turn, sends items based on their understanding of the case. Possible cognitive bias effects are already in play before the evidence has even arrived at the forensic lab.

Let's return for a moment to Anderson's experiment with fire investigation and the copper beads, which we discussed earlier under expectation bias. Did Anderson find his results because he expected to see them (expectation bias), or did he find evidence to confirm his theory while ignoring the obvious issues concerning the solubility of molten metals (confirmation bias)? Did he rely too heavily on a notion that the molten metal would display different compositions depending on when the

---

[29] I.E. Dror et al., 'Letter to the Editor—Context Management Toolbox: A Linear Sequential Unmasking (LSU) Approach for Minimizing Cognitive Bias in Forensic Decision Making', *Journal of Forensic Science* 60(4) (2015).

electrical arc that formed the bead occurred (anchoring bias)? Or did he have information from someone else that swayed the basis of his whole research (contextual bias)?

Expectation, confirmation, anchoring, and contextual biases are very much intermingled, and it may not be possible to untangle them. That said, does it really matter which one it was? I would argue that the answer is a resounding 'no'. What is important to understand is that *all* of them can impede open-minded decision making.

- **E. *Role effects*** are where scientists identify themselves within adversarial judicial systems as part of either the prosecution or defence teams. This may introduce subconscious bias that can influence decisions, especially where some ambiguity exists.

It used to be that scientists would attend crime scenes and meetings, and generally engage in a dialogue with the police about what to submit and what not to. Privatisation placed labs a step further away from the police. What usually happens now is that someone from the police will determine what to send for external forensic analysis. This approach softens the impact of role-effect coming from the lab-based scientists.

The role of the police isn't to spend time looking for innocent people; their role is to prevent crime, and, if one occurs, find the criminal. However, from time to time, the police will end up building a case against the wrong person. Even when this is alleged (such as the defendant insisting they are innocent), the options may not bifurcate neatly into continuing to investigate the suspect whilst looking at whether it could be someone else.

As mentioned earlier, the items sent for forensic analysis are determined largely by the police or the SSM, based on what they are trying to prove. What the forensic scientist sees will still be a set of evidence that is on one side of the scales of justice, and they won't know about any potential evidence which might undermine the allegation. In other words, there is a risk that pre-selection of evidence by a prosecuting body will miss or ignore any exculpatory evidence.

Twenty years ago, dialogue existed between lab experts and the police regarding how best to tackle the evidence and explore issues, which ultimately assisted both the prosecution and the defence. These days, it often falls to defence experts to undertake selection and analysis of items that really should have been done by the police and their agents. Defence experts have ended up becoming entrenched in the investigation, sometimes revealing evidence that thrusts a case firmly into reverse.

In one case, a man was arrested for setting fire to his own ground-floor flat. Nothing had been taken, but several rooms were set on fire with surprisingly little damage. It looked like someone had poured a highly volatile liquid such as lighter fluid or isopropyl alcohol on the lounge carpet, down the hallway, and around the bed in the single bedroom.

The fire was discovered around 10:00AM. By the time the fire service got there, it had almost subsided, save for the smouldering mattress. The occupant (who had the only key) had left an hour earlier, and the flat was secure according to the firefighters who had to open the windows.

It seems like a straightforward case, except the suspect was clear that he didn't do it. The case rolled on towards trial despite one obvious question: how had the fire burned for an hour when no one had noticed any smoke before 10:00AM? The flat was at street level, next to a road in a busy city suburb with plenty of foot traffic. The suspect also had a steady job and no house insurance.

The suspect's own evidence was that he left a window ajar on a latch for ventilation. Significantly, the person who reported the fire at 10:00AM said in a statement that he had seen smoke coming from an *open window* in the lounge. Despite this, the prosecution maintained the flat had been secure (and that, by inference, no-one had broken in to set it on fire).

The CSI must have considered the possibility of a break-in, since they had taken the time to fingerprint the outside of the windows. Out of prudence and concern for the case, another fingerprint expert and

I checked the work that had been done. It was only as a result of a visit to the police fingerprint department that we found two other CSI fingerprint lifts, which had *not* been mentioned in the notes or statements or shown in any photographs. The marks themselves were smudged and useless for fingerprint comparison, but their patterns did show one thing: that someone had climbed in through the ground floor window—the same one smoke was seen coming from.

Why wasn't this served or mentioned? At the very least, the CSIs would have known these were 'peeper' or 'burglar' marks, as they are called. They should have flagged this, but doing so would have meant conceding that the officer-in-charge had the wrong person. Could cognitive bias from role effects have been a factor in how the marks came to be ignored? There was little doubt that someone else had set fire to the flat sometime after the tenant had left for work, but they were wrongly targeted as a suspect despite written evidence from a witness and physical evidence from a CSI.

- **F. *Motivational bias*** occurs where, for example, motivational influence on decision making results in information consistent with a favoured conclusion tending to be subject to a lower level of scrutiny than information that may support a less favoured outcome.

If you've read this several times, you might, like me, still be wondering what it means. In short, it's the subtle bias of arriving at a result even if there isn't much support for it. In civil cases, where some experts are very mindful of keeping their clients happy, bending the truth slightly is sometimes a way of walking the line between ethical and unethical behaviour. The trouble is, if you know you're pushing your luck with a theory that isn't supported just because it is favourable, then that isn't cognitive bias. That's just bias.

In a prominent multiple fatality fire in the UK, the Crown produced something called 'petrol additive' evidence. You might expect that fire debris can be examined to look for things like traces of petrol, which can linger far longer and more resiliently than most people would expect.

Despite a raging fire and layers of charred wood, blackened plastics, and twisted metal, petrol residue can still be there. But there is a limit: petrol residue does continue to degrade and evaporate, and, over time, dissipates to an unidentifiable level.

One company took the initiative to look for petrol additives in the debris. These are additives that the likes of major petrol brands put into their products to help keep the engine clean and lubricated. They tend to be massively complex mixtures that stick around after the petrol has long evaporated, although washing tends to remove them. The finding of such residues in debris and clothing can be said to show that there was contact with a particular brand of petrol at some point.

Evidence in the trial included a variety of clothing and fire debris samples, with varying amounts of petrol found on some, but only petrol additives on others.

One of the prosecution experts did some further work on this area using a new, adapted technique. I won't go into the chemistry behind it, but he produced a report stating that he had found petrol additives in a particular and very relevant sample of fire debris. Most fire debris is so complex that careful analysis of "negative" and petrol additive-spiked debris is needed to determine if the technique can distinguish a petrol additive from the mishmash of chemical rubbish. Without this background validation work, the chemist can't tell if any results are real or just shapes in the chemical clouds.

In this case, the expert had failed to appreciate how complex fire debris can be and hadn't run any negative controls (samples of fire debris with no petrol additive in them). When this was pointed out, he took the initiative to undertake more tests, eventually realising that his original findings could be a false positive. He retracted his statement ahead of the trial, and the jury were none the wiser.

This is a good example of what can be achieved when experts from each side can get together in an open and non-contentious setting. However, in terms of how the initial statement came about: it wasn't money, and it wasn't ego. I genuinely believe the prosecution expert was trying to be helpful (role bias or motivational bias), which drove the initial presumptive, but unfortunately unsupported, findings.

- **G. *Reconstructive effects*** can occur when people rely on memory rather than taking contemporaneous notes. In this case people tend subsequently to to fill in gaps with what they believe should have happened, and so may be influenced by protocol requirements when recalling events some time later from memory.

This is perhaps the most common and well-known area of cognitive bias. As discussed earlier, witness recollections are notorious for leading cases astray.

In England, Wales and Northern Ireland, experts are not expected to remember everything they documented. If they are unable to recall something from memory while in the witness box, they can simply ask the judge if they may refer to their notes. (The exception to this is Scotland, where referring to notes on the stand is not allowed unless the notes have been previously served as an exhibit called a Production.)

This does, however, rely on experts making detailed and accurate notes. Forensic experts using accredited methods will have their notes set out to the minimum required standard, but outside of this, it can be highly variable. Even with detailed notes, failing to refer to them when writing a report or preparing for trial might leave you with the wrong thing stuck in your head. In the worst case scenario, the inaccurate memory can be transposed into a report without checking for any notes or photographs that contradict it.

Cognitive bias is now the dish of the day in forensics. Time and money have been poured into research on how its effects can be minimised. After all, you want your forensic experts to be unbiased, and not let external or internal experiences, information, or prejudices affect the way a case is analysed and reported. Yet even that can fail.

In one case where a person was doused with corrosive liquid, neither myself nor the Crown's scientist were given any context such as the witness statements. Somehow, we both ended up creating what we thought had happened, believing that we had read it somewhere, when in fact neither of us had been given any information of the sort. We had both subconsciously made up different accounts of events.

To reiterate: context is what makes forensic science different from just 'science'. By micromanaging context, you can end up with massive backlogs, cherry-picked evidence, scientists who make their own assumptions, or results which have been interpreted by people who are unqualified to do so and end up turning the whole thing on its head.

Understanding the types, risks, and occurrences of cognitive bias is arguably a better way forward than trying to limit and control the context. Depending on the approach taken, it will mitigate things to some degree, but can only go so far. If you want a quality check on the forensic evidence, including a cognitive bias assessment, then I can give you an easy way to do it: turn it over to the dark side. That's right—have one of us look at it. If there's an issue, there's a good chance we'll find it.

Non-Cognitive Bias (AKA: Bias)

There are people who deliberately distort the criminal justice system. We've seen cases like the one where a police officer claimed to have been attacked from behind by a knife, though it was obvious his jacket had been cut with a pair of scissors. A Forensic Science Service (FSS) scientist once joked with me that they knew when the police had egged the evidence, as they would get a request to look for 'traces of glass' and find a handful of the stuff in the pocket of the garment. Staffordshire and Cleveland Police had to review 355 cases over a 15-year period when they found out one of their officers had lied about his qualifications and given evidence outside his area of expertise.[1]

The Independent Office for Police Conduct (IOPC), formerly the Independent Police Complaints Commission, routinely investigates allegations of corruption, including problems like the ones above. Ironically, in 2018, this included investigation into the Met's own anti-corruption unit.[2]

When you consider how many officers might be affected by corruption, disinterest, lack of training and so on, this ultimately affects the quality of evidence-gathering, however unintentionally. While many cases involve forensic and eyewitness evidence, with funding drying up, more concessions and compromises in terms of service levels are inevitable. If support, infrastructure and–perhaps above all–boots on the ground fall, the job for the investigating bodies, especially the police, only gets harder and harder while morale drops.

Coupled with the squeeze on the CPS and the courts pushing for early listings, it's no surprise that even though serious crimes have

---

[1] 'IPCC Reviews Stephen Beattie 'Botched' Police Case', *BBC News* (14 June 2013). Available at https://www.bbc.co.uk/news/uk-england-22910279.

[2] V. Dodd, 'Metropolitan Police's Anti-Corruption Unit Faces Investigation', *The Guardian* (22 July 2018). Available at https://www.theguardian.com/uk-news/2018/jul/22/metropolitan-police-anti-corruption-unit-faces-investigation.

been on the rise,[3] the number of cases before the courts has been falling.[4]

There is, however, a grey area between unintentional (cognitive) bias and plain, old-fashioned lying. It's non-cognitive-but-not-quite-lying bias, or, as I call it (if only so I don't have to keep typing the whole thing): non-cognitive bias.

At this stage, we need to consider how prosecution and defence services are funded. In England and Wales, the police are largely responsible for the acquisition of forensic services: any tasks which can be done in-house will be done in-house, failing which they are sent to external forensic labs, such as Eurofins, Cellmark and Key Forensics. Unsurprisingly, as police budgets were slashed, their spending on forensic services got lower and lower each time an external contract came up for bidding. In 2019, a House of Lords Select Committee report found that forensic spending fell from £120 million in 2008 to around £50–£55 million in 2018–2019.[5]

With spending dropping year by year, the police fought for cheaper contracts, resulting in economic carnage: in order to win contracts, forensic labs ended up cutting their bid prices below what was needed to keep them afloat. This culminated with Key Forensics going into administration in 2018,[6] and all three major forensic service providers gave evidence to the House of Lords that they were struggling to remain profitable.

---

[3] J. Sligo, *Case Volumes Falling off a Cliff Despite Rise in Serious Crime,* The Law Soc Gazette News (3 July 2019). Available at https://www.lawgazette.co.uk/news/case-volumes-falling-off-a-cliff-despite-rise-in-serious-crime/5070836.article.

[4] Office of National Statistics, *Crime in England and Wales: Year Ending March 2019* (18 July 2019). Available at https://www.ons.gov.uk/peoplepopulationandcommunity/crimeandjustice/bulletins/crimeinenglandandwales/yearendingmarch2019.

[5] House of Lords Science and Technology Select Committee, *Forensic Science and the Criminal Justice System: A Blueprint for Change*, HL Paper 333, UK Parliament (1 May 2019). Available at https://publications.parliament.uk/pa/ld201719/ldselect/ldsctech/333/33302.htm.

[6] Parliamentary Question by D. Hanson, *Key Forensic Services: Insolvency* (UIN 127023), UK Parliament (answered 14 February 2018). Available at https://www.parliament.uk/business/publications/written-questions-answers-statements/written-question/Commons/2018-02-06/127023/.

Moreover, defence work is funded primarily through Legal Aid, which has faced its own share of budget issues. Various providers raised concerns over inadequate Legal Aid funding before the House of Lords, with one noting that current hourly rates for most disciplines are now *less* than what they were in 1999.[7] Amongst many other recommendations, the Select Committee report noted that "[f]air access to justice for defendants is further hampered by cuts to legal aid."

In a formal response to the Select Committee report, the government recognised the need for action and ways of sustaining provision of forensic services to the police.[8]

"The Committee report rightly identifies instability within the forensics market as an important issue," they noted. However, in regard to defence work and Legal Aid, they added, "[t]he government is not aware of legally aided defendants being denied access to forensic testing and expert advice for funding reasons."

Legal Aid funding isn't adjusted for inflation, and so it's worth a few percent less each year. While adjustments were made to make prosecution labs sustainable, nothing has been done to assist Legal Aid funding, on top of the looming spectre of upcoming mandatory accreditation requirements. Despite the number of cases in which defence experts have prevented an innocent person being sent to jail, the scales of funding for forensic services provision in England and Wales have tipped in favour of the prosecution.

This is what I mean by non-cognitive bias. Here is an avoidable, but sustained, weakening of the defence: slowly pulling the funding foundation from under it whilst bolstering the prosecution.

---

[7] Ibid.

[8] *Government Response to the Lords Science and Technology Select Committee Report,* UK Parliament (July 2019). Available at https://www.parliament.uk/globalassets/documents/lords-committees/science-technology/forensic-science/Govt-response-forensic-science.pdf.

There are other core forensic issues that play into non-cognitive bias. One of them is the use of likelihood ratios for several forensic disciplines, along with their accompanying scales of support.

Consider FSR-G-222, the official guidance on DNA Mixture Interpretation issued by the Forensic Science Regulator (FSR).[9] As a guidance document, it is intended for use by practitioners, though it is possible that it may be referred to in court. In other words, it isn't exactly optional, and you can expect some kind of backlash should you choose to go against it.

By way of background, DNA analysis uses a statistical figure to express a degree of confidence in results, known as the likelihood ratio. In its simplest form, it is the ratio of the probability that an observed DNA result contains, for example, my DNA profile versus the probability that the DNA profile belongs to someone else. If the likelihood ratio is exactly 1, then the findings do not support one proposition over the other. If it's >1, this supports the proposition that I was the contributor of the DNA profile. A ratio <1 supports the proposition that I was not.

DNA has become more and more sensitive, allowing for analysis of poor quality and/or low quantity DNA which was previously impossible. Consequently, the interpretation of DNA data has become more and more complex, and the tools DNA experts use to evaluate and interpret DNA data has had to evolve.

Probabilistic genotyping (PG) was introduced in the mid-2000s as a method for interpreting the new complexities.[10] Interpretation guidelines

---

[9] Forensic Science Regulator, *Forensic Science Regulator Guidance: DNA Mixture Interpretation FSR-G-222* (2020). Available at https://www.gov.uk/government/publications/dna-mixture-interpretation-fsr-g-222.

[10] The SWGDAM Interpretation Guidelines for Autosomal STR Typing by Forensic DNA Testing Laboratories defines PG as "the use of biological modeling, statistical theory, computer algorithms, and probability distributions to calculate likelihood ratios (LRs) and/or infer genotypes" (as at 13 July 2021).

regarding its use were subsequently published by the Scientific Working Group on DNA Analysis Methods (SWGDAM).[11]

In 2012, an international conference was held in Rome specifically to address the challenges scientists faced with complex DNA mixtures.[12] Specialised software makes it possible to generate statistics from low levels of and/or degraded DNA, even within complex mixtures that previously precluded interpretation.

The FSR recommendation is to express a likelihood ratio where possible. If there is no statistical basis, then, in England and Wales, the Court of Appeal ruling in *R v. Dlugosz* allows DNA evidence to be expressed with an evaluative opinion,[13] provided a) it is clear that there is no statistical basis; and b) the expert has a proper basis for giving their evaluation.

The European Network of Forensic Science Institutes (ENFSI) guidelines for evaluative reporting use a scale which converts the likelihood ratio to verbal expressions of support, as seen in the following:[14]

LR	Level of Support
2–10	Weak support
10–100	Moderate support
100–1000	Moderately strong support

---

[11] SWGDAM Interpretation Guidelines for Autosomal STR Typing by Forensic DNA Testing Laboratories, approved 1/14/10.

[12] *The Hidden Side of DNA Profiles: Artifacts, Errors and Uncertain Evidence*, International Conference in Rome, Italy (27–28 April 2012).

[13] *R v. Dlugosz and Ors* (2013) EWCA Crim 2.

[14] European Network of Forensic Science Institutes, *Guideline for Evaluative Reporting in Forensic Science* (2015). Available at https://enfsi.eu/wp-content/uploads/2016/09/m1_guideline.pdf.

1000–10k	Strong support
10k–1 million	Very strong support
>1 million	Extremely strong support

There are two problems with using a verbal scale.

The first is the inherent assumption that a lay person will grasp what each of the levels really means. A further study of verbal scales by Martire and Watkins found that "…if the intention of verbal conclusion scales is to facilitate effective and accurate communication of opinions regarding evidential weight, then that aim has not been achieved."[15] It concludes: "[T[he verbal conclusion scales do not appear to fulfil the purpose of assisting the court or facilitating effective and accurate communication."

The second problem is that this structure does not give an option for 'unable to tell'; there's no level for 'probably best not to guess'. The whole scale, whether you use the LR or its written equivalents, is founded on the principle that as long as it's >1, there is some level of support.

To understand why this becomes an issue with DNA analysis, you first need to understand DNA mixture and/or partial profile analysis. If you are a DNA analyst, please feel free skip the next few paragraphs. Otherwise, read on:

Imagine my DNA profile is a 17-piece jigsaw puzzle of the Eiffel Tower. Then, imagine a complainant's DNA profile as also being a jigsaw puzzle of the Eiffel Tower, but viewed from a different direction. If you took both puzzles and mixed the pieces up, it would still be relatively easy to separate them and say which jigsaw was whose. This is the equivalent

---

[15] K.A. Martire and I. Watkins, 'Perception Problems of the Verbal Scale: A Reanalysis and Application of a Membership Function Approach', *Science & Justice* 55 264–273 (2015). Available at https://doi.org/10.1016/j.scijus.2015.01.002.

of a simple mixture, where both DNA profiles are of good quality and in high quantities.

Now let's mix them up again, this time using all of the complainant's pieces but only ten of mine. You can see how separating the two would be trickier: although you could reform the complainant's entire jigsaw, the missing seven pieces mean you would have to make assumptions about mine, though you might still feel you have enough to be able to make a call.

Now let's take ten pieces of the complainant's jigsaw, five of mine, and add in pieces from one to three other people's jigsaws (also of the Eiffel Tower, and taken from different views). How do you know if the pieces you have selected belong to the complainant, me, or one of the others?

To add to this, imagine using a type of software that can decide whether or not to ignore pieces when it finds them. You can usually determine how many other people's jigsaws were added to the mix, which limits the number of options, but a colleague has seen cases where the number of contributors was incorrect.

What if you accidentally took a piece believing it came from my jigsaw when it was really from an unrelated one? In the worst case scenario, what if there were actually *no* pieces from my jigsaw—but because you thought mine was part of the mix, you accidentally took several pieces from each of the other contributors' jigsaws, and made something that looked like pieces from mine?

Welcome to complex DNA mixture analysis: it is theoretically possible to assign a positive likelihood for a DNA profile of someone who *isn't in the mixture*.

In the US, this issue was flagged in the 2016 President's Council of Advisors on Science and Technology (PCAST) report. The report noted that advances in programmes for interpreting complex mixtures, such as STRmix™, have helped move the discipline away from what are, in essence, educated guesses. However, it continued, "[T]hey still require scientific scrutiny, however, to determine (1) whether the methods are scientifically valid, including defining the limitations on their reliability (that is, the circumstances in which they may yield unreliable results) and (2) whether the software correctly implements the methods."[16] The report recommended that the validity of these methods be limited to a three-contributor mixture (i.e. a three-jigsaw mixture) of a sufficient DNA level and with a minor proportion of at least 20%.

The forensic DNA community responded quite strongly to this (unsurprisingly, as STRmix™ is used by many organisations). They produced a joint summary that provided strong support for STRmix™'s discriminatory abilities in mixtures with three to five contributors.[17]

The fact STRmix™ can do what it does is a mathematical marvel, but it was put to the test by a team from the government lab at Sciences Judiciaires et Médicine Légale in Montreal.[18] They took four mixtures and compared them with virtual DNA profiles generated by sampling of actual DNA information (i.e. fake people who were not contributors to the DNA mixtures).

The Montreal team found a high degree of support for STRmix™ to distinguish DNA mixtures out of the millions of comparisons done. The largest estimated LR for a non-contributor (i.e. a false positive) was 43,238 for the mixtures generated in-house and 17,200 for the casework mixtures. Both of these ratios are 'Very Strong Support' on the ENFSI scale for a contributor who was *not* present in the mixture.

---

[16] President's Council of Advisors on Science and Technology, *Report to the President, Forensic Science in Criminal Courts: Ensuring Scientific Validity of Feature-Comparison Methods* (September 2016). Available at https://obamawhitehouse.archives.gov/sites/default/files/microsites/ostp/PCAST/pcast_forensic_science_report_final.pdf.

[17] J.A. Bright et al., 'Internal Validation of STRmix™—A Multi Laboratory Response to PCAST', *Forensic Science International: Genetics* 34 11–24 (2018). Available at https://doi.org10.1016/j.fsigen.2018.01.003.

[18] S. Noel et al., 'STRmix™ Put to the Test: 300 000 Non-Contributor Profiles Compared to Four Contributor DNA Mixtures and the Impact of Replicates', *Forensic Science International: Genetics* 41 24–31 (2019). Available at https://doi.org/10.1016/j.fsigen.2019.03.017.

Their analysis found that of the 7.2 million comparisons made, "only a low proportion (0.9%) of the non-contributor comparisons returned false H_1 support comparisons" (i.e. a false positive). Put another way, there were 64,800 false positive results where the answer was at least 'Weak support'; of these, over 6,000 were 'Moderate support'. What this shows is the realistic potential for false inclusions in complex DNA mixtures.

False positives, however, aren't captured by the likelihood ratio system. In other words, it is acceptable to express 'moderate support' for someone's DNA matching the one in the sample, even though there might not be a match. To guard against this, some laboratories have a threshold below which they will report findings as 'inconclusive',[19] but this is not universal. Similar concerns have been raised on social media by Gerhard, an Australian forensic DNA consultant.[20]

Paradoxically, the more sensitive our techniques become, the higher the chance of detecting background DNA unrelated to an incident—and, therefore, that false positives may arise.

This plays directly into the issues of cognitive bias and the same problems discussed earlier, where uncertainty, bias, and confidence can lead to problems with eyewitness evidence. Scientists, much as they recognise the power of technology like STRmix™, also understand the strengths and weaknesses of the likelihood scale. But consider the following hypothetical example of what can happen outside that bubble:

A sexual assault allegation follows from at a party in Clacton, and the assailant is an unknown male. The complainant's description is poor, but she remembers a man putting his hand down her underwear; while she tried to fight him off, someone heard the commotion and he ran

---

[19] For example, for complex mixtures, the LR or its verbal scale would be referred to only if the LR was >10,000 and not >1. A LR between 1 and 10,000 would be inconclusive.

[20] J. Gerhard, 'The Verbal Scale for DNA Evidence and Why It Is No Longer Fit for Purpose', *LinkedIn post* (4 May 2020). Available at https://www.linkedin.com/pulse/verbal-scale-dna-evidence-why-longer-fit-purpose-jae-gerhard/.

off. Swabs and tapings are taken from the underwear and skin surfaces and sent for DNA analysis, along with reference samples from men present at the party, one of whom is Schudel.

The DNA report comes back indicating 'weak support' that Schudel's DNA is present in the mixture. The detective investigating the case hones in on Schudel, and finds that he has a previous arrest and conviction for something unrelated. Schudel is arrested and interviewed regarding the alleged assault.

Schudel is repeatedly asked what happened at that party that night, but maintains that he has no idea and that he had stayed downstairs. The detective counters that a forensic report found his DNA on the complainant's underwear.

In desperation, Schudel suggests that they might have sat on the same seat at some point. This explanation is put to a DNA expert, who dismisses it. Of the two versions of events—namely, that Schudel had intimate contact with the complainant, or that the DNA on her underwear came from sitting on the same seat—the defence account does not appear to be credible. This, in turn, makes the prosecution case seem stronger.

Here we have *uncertainty* (the weak DNA result), *bias* (Schudel has a criminal history and was at the party) and *confidence* (the explanation Schudel gave wasn't credible), which, put together, land Schudel in the dock, accused of something he didn't do. However, one obvious possibility hasn't been raised at all: weak support simply might mean it wasn't his DNA. Would a jury fully appreciate the difference between 'weak support' and 'it's DNA evidence, so it *has* to be him'?

I would argue that anything under a LR of 10—and possibly even as high as 100—should be automatically deemed 'inconclusive', given the results of the Montreal study. In practice, some DNA labs have adopted a cut-off LR where it becomes too risky to provide an opinion for results under a certain threshold, though this is not a requirement.

The ENFSI likelihood scale doesn't just apply to DNA. It is commonly used in various forensic disciplines, such as examining documents, fibres, glass, and imagery comparisons. Although its guidelines encourage care in using the scale, it does not define 'inconclusive' other than when the balance of probabilities is exactly 1. The guidelines even warn that 'weak support' for one proposition should not be misinterpreted as conveying strong support for an alternative proposition,[21] further bolstering the notion that 'weak support' has clear evidential value.

Ironically, despite my earlier comments about the poor reporting structure for fingerprint comparisons, those at least have defined categories of 'insufficient' and 'inconclusive'. Verbal scales of weak support (2–10) or even moderate support (10–100) can sway a lay person into believing that evidence has significant merit when the results may have no value at all. Such approaches bake 'non-cognitive bias' into the system.

Against this backdrop of how cases fail and why a defence expert review is important, we will now step back to 1990—and take our first steps into the dark side.

---

[21] European Network of Forensic Science Institutes, *Guideline for Evaluative Reporting in Forensic Science* (2015). Available at https://enfsi.eu/wp-content/uploads/2016/09/m1_guideline.pdf.

IIDs and Offices Don't Mix

You might be familiar with the IED, or improvised explosive device, but there is also the IID: the improvised incendiary device. These devices, which range from the basic to the sophisticated, are used to start fires in various ways. In the 1990s, the Animal Liberation Front (ALF) was doing exactly that.

A security guard in a fur coat warehouse found such a device, which had been placed there with the sole purpose of burning the warehouse to the ground. Put aside any personal thoughts you might have about fur: a building on fire endangers not only the public, but the firefighters who risk their lives to put the fire out. When the suspected ALF activists were arrested, the court needed to determine whether the device would have started a fire.

The device was simple enough: two 4-litre plastic cola bottles filled with petrol and strapped to an ignitor, made from a chemical mixture, a light bulb, and a delay set with a clockwork timer. The only real way to check whether such a device would have worked was by building one. Reconstruction is one of the cornerstones of forensic science–and arguably one of the most fun.

In the early 1990s, at Keith Borer Consultants' (KBC) little office atop the hill at Durham University, we didn't exactly have a testing space for the ad-hoc and slightly chaotic experiments we ended up doing. We had either an office floor or Dr. Borer's house. When it came to reconstructing the devices, I wasn't crazy enough to fill the bottles with petrol, but the ignition mixture alone burned a fiery hole through the plastic, at which point I knew we'd seen enough. The devices would work.

These days I would have a heart attack if I saw the foolish things I got up to back then in the name of forensic science, made more ironic by the fact that I often wrote opinions in health and safety cases. Overall—and with a little planning—luck prevailed: I only singed my eyebrows once. (I was electrocuted another time, but that was me trying to figure out why the large scientific oven wouldn't switch on and had nothing to do with case work.) I also almost set the office on fire, something a colleague eventually managed to do years later, and Dr. Borer almost had his head taken off in a pressure cooker experiment.

In the early 1990s, there had been a spate of letter-bombs in the news. These were plain, brown-paper-wrapped video (VHS) tapes, which fit through a letterbox. Thanks to some good detective work, the maker was tracked down, arrested and charged under the Explosives Act. His barrister, however, pointed out: how did we know the devices were dangerous? His defence was that the letter-bombs were nuisance devices designed to scare people, not IEDs.

I can see how, at this point, many readers might think this really didn't matter; if someone was posting anything like this through letterboxes, we should throw the book at them all the same. Nonetheless, that's not how the law works: the punishment must fit the crime. Would we charge someone who fired an air rifle in public with the same offence as someone who had fired a machine gun? In one case, a grandmother was fined £150 for littering as she fed a piece of sausage roll to a pigeon.[1] Was that proportionate? When dealing with defence cases, the question of whether the charge matches the crime is one area that experts invariably find themselves involved with.

In the letter-bombs case, the devices had been placed inside a VHS video box. For those of you who don't know what that is—which I know is a good chunk of society these days—it's basically a plastic folding case, about the size of a book, that snaps shut. The recipient would receive a wrapped parcel containing a black VHS case, which they would open expecting to find a video tape.

According to the Crown, what followed at this stage would have been a life-threatening explosion. The defendant was adamant that this wasn't

---

[1] 'Woman Fined £150 for Feeding Pigeon Sausage Roll in Bath', *BBC News* (19 June 2019). Available at https://www.bbc.com/news/uk-england-somerset-48692073.

true, and said all it would have done was make a loud bang. Once again, there was only one way to find out.

I collected the components, which were mechanical in nature: a clothes peg, nail, shotgun cartridge (with the shot removed) and tape. Perched in the middle of the office floor, I carefully assembled the device, primed the clothes peg, and closed the VHS box. Just as the device was armed and ready, a man in a Fire Service uniform appeared in the doorway.

"Don't mind me," he said cheerfully, as I sat hunched precariously over an ominous-looking box. "I'm just doing the fire inspection."

Off he went around the office, checking the fire extinguishers, until he finally came back to where he'd started. "All good!" he chirped, and was gone.

It was ten minutes before we stopped laughing. I then sat down with my VHS case and opened the lid.

There was a 'whoosh' and a pop: not just a bang, but also not quite a fireball. The device was relatively benign unless you opened it close to your face, in which case the damage could have been a lot worse. Nonetheless, it would be impossible to control who might open the package, or how. As counsel later argued: what if the recipient's six-year-old son had been the one to find the package, held it up, and peeked inside? The client pleaded guilty.

As though to prove the point, I eventually decided to get rid of the excess propellant left over from the reconstruction by putting it on the pavement outside and setting fire to it. As I lit it, I leaned over the little pyramid I had created, and that was when my eyebrows got singed.

Blowing things up wasn't just limited to the world of IIDs. We had a client who supplied fizzy pop in glass bottles (the kind that used to be delivered by the milkman, if you're old enough to remember that).

The company was occasionally sued by people who claimed that bottles had exploded while they were holding/lifting/sitting next to them.

The pattern of damage to the glass in a bottle is very different if it explodes as a result of being struck from the outside as opposed to excessive internal pressure. However, as good as the literature on this was, it was far better to try it yourself and have reference samples. It was easy enough to knock bottles off tables and floors to show how they looked when struck from the outside, but how do you simulate what a glass fizzy pop bottle would look like if it exploded due to an excessive build-up of internal pressure? To my chemistry-addled brain, the obvious answer seemed to be to empty out the liquid and put a decent firework inside.

To retain the glass pieces so that I could study the damage patterns, I wrapped the bottle with clear sticky tape several times, and then—just in case that didn't work—swaddled the bottle in a heavy cotton blackout cloth. I put the whole thing in our hazardous test facility (i.e. the men's toilet), popped a large banger type firework inside the glass bottle, lit it, folded the blackout cloth over the bottle and retreated to a safe distance (i.e. the office next to the toilet).

After a few seconds, there was a loud 'phoop', and I opened the toilet door to a haze of smoke. I carefully opened the blackout cloth to find the bottle still very much intact…but the cloth itself on fire.

I beat out the fire and tried again, only to find the blackout cloth was, once again, on fire. I put out the flames and waited. A few seconds later, a flame randomly popped up on the cloth. I smothered it and another appeared in a different spot. Sensing this wasn't going well, I ran the entire cloth under the sink until it was completely wet. Two tries later, I still had one fully intact glass bottle and a blackout cloth that looked like moths had been at it. It then occurred to me I could just fill the bottle with water, seal the top, and freeze it. The next day, I had my broken bottle.

These early years were a range of weird and interesting cases, with a freedom in forensics that you just don't see anymore. But of them all, nothing quite beats the Euromac case: the sale of what was purportedly nuclear weapon parts to Iraq. Before we get to that, however, it might be useful to consider the story of Gerald Bull and the Supergun.

In the 1960s, if you wanted to fire something from a cannon further than anyone else, Gerald Bull was the person to ask.[2] Born in Canada, his lifelong goal was to be able to put a satellite into orbit, not by using a rocket, but by firing it from a giant cannon.

Although he built artillery for the US, Bull struggled to get funding for the project of his dreams, right up until Saddam Hussein heard about his abilities and offered him the opportunity of a lifetime: to build a 'Supergun'.

Project Babylon, as it came to be called, was slated to be 150m (495ft) long, with a 1m (3.3ft) wide barrel. A scaled-down version of the gun had already been built and test-fired. This was 106m (350ft) long, and two more were in the making.

The barrel of the Supergun was made in the UK by Sheffield Forgemasters, who had been told it was for a petroleum pipeline. Eight sections of the supposed pipe were stopped at Teesside on 8 April 1990, en route to being shipped to Iraq.[3] Two Forgemasters employees were arrested for violating an embargo on arms sales.

It was later revealed that both the Ministry of Defence (MOD) and the Department of Trade and Industry (later replaced by the Department for Innovation, Universities and Skills and Department for Business, Enterprise and Regulatory Reform) had known about the proposed

---

[2] W. Lowther, *Iraq and the Supergun: Gerald Bull — The True Story of Saddam Hussein's Dr Doom* (Pan Books, 1992).

[3] 'On this Day', *BBC News* (11 April 1990). Available at http://news.bbc.co.uk/onthisday/hi/dates/stories/april/11/newsid_2477000/2477023.stm.

project and sale of the pipe sections to Iraq, because Forgemasters had contacted them about their concerns, but neither agency blocked the sale. To top it all off, shortly before the discovery, Gerald Bull had been assassinated outside his apartment in Brussels on 22 March that same year. It was the stuff spy movies are made of (and indeed became the subject of a movie eventually).[4]

Firing a gun this big requires something more than standard powder charges. Normally, a block of powder is placed in the base of the gun and ignited, and off the projectile goes. Massively long barrels, however, need something to compensate for the amount of time it takes the powder to burn through.

One of Gerald Bull's much earlier guns, the 36m (119ft) long, 40cm (16in) wide High Altitude Research Project (HARP), used a powder charge that was almost 3.6m (12ft) long.[5] In order to improve the ignition, the charge was split into different sections, with each section then ignited simultaneously in what is known as multiple-point ignition. One can only guess the size of the charge used for the Supergun (a BBC article mentions nine tonnes, although the source isn't given).[6] Igniting this using multi-point ignition would have required some very fast timers and switches. This is where we come to Euromac.

In 1991, Ali Daghir, an Iraqi man, and Jeanine Speckman, a French woman, the directors of UK-based Euromac, were charged with conspiracy to export 40 electrical capacitors to Iraq. The charges came after a joint Central Intelligence Agency (CIA) and MI5/MI6 operation following the trail of said capacitors, which they believed were to be used to make a nuclear weapon. The Crown was quite specific that the devices could only be used to make a nuclear weapon, and had *no other* non-military use.

---

[4]   R. Young (dir.), *Doomsday Gun* (Griffin Productions and HBO Showcase, 1994).

[5]   NASA, N67-35604, *Scientific and Technical Aerospace Reports*, 5(21) (1967).

[6]   W. Park, 'The Tragic Tale of Saddam Hussein's 'Supergun', *BBC News* (18 March 2016). Available at https://www.bbc.com/future/article/20160317-the-man-who-tried-to-make-a-supergun-for-saddam-hussein.

This is where the case landed at KBC. I can only imagine that phone call. Who else, however, would the Crown have approached? It's not like there was a string of ex-nuclear-bomb-makers advertising their expert witness credentials in the 1990s (nor is there one now). I suspect KBC got the call because our company had a record of dealing with terrorist cases, but it didn't mean we had any idea about nuclear weapons. However, if the only choices were having a scientist look at the case versus having no-one look at it, then, to use a metaphor from the car industry: some grease is better than no grease.

At first sight, the case was heavily tipped in favour of the Crown. All but two of their expert statements made similar declarations to the extent that the capacitors were "military specification" and "consistent with a capacitor used in a firing set for nuclear weapons," despite the fact, much like us at KBC, all but two of the experts were engineers and had no more idea how to make a nuclear weapon than we did.

One UK expert acting on behalf of the Ministry of Defence (MOD) who examined the items stated that he believed the capacitor had been specifically designed for military use.[7] I wonder, though, if he could have been expected to say anything else. It's classic cognitive bias: if you work for an organisation whose entire function is military by nature, then that's all you know.

What I *did* know was that any electrical capacitor with an operational range that barely goes below 0°C is hardly going to work in a nuclear warhead strapped to a military aircraft at 12,000m (40,000ft). In short, they weren't military-grade—at least not if you wanted to fly or use one on a cold night, despite what most of the so-called experts had said.

What was also hard to get my head round was this: despite the claims that the capacitors had no civilian purpose, we had a drawer full of them at my university research laboratory. We used the same type of capacitors

---

[7] Department of Trade and Industry, *Report of the Inquiry into the Export of Defence Equipment and Dual-use Goods to Iraq and Related Prosecutions (Scott Inquiry),* Her Majesty's Stationery Office (National Archives, UK) (1996). Available at https://discovery.nationalarchives.gov.uk/details/r/C188.

to synchronise lasers. In essence, they were very fast and accurate switches of the sort you might use in niche research, as we had done. It did occur to me that they could be used to simultaneously ignite a multiple-point powder charge at the base of a supergun. Either way, they certainly had more uses than making a nuclear weapon.

You might be thinking: does it matter if the capacitors were intended for a supergun or a nuclear bomb? That's exactly how the law works: the pair who were arrested were specifically charged with selling items to Iraq to make a nuclear weapon, so if this wasn't true, there would be no case to answer. However, the judge directed the jury that they could convict even if they thought the devices were not for a nuclear bomb but a military purpose. As a result, both the Euromac directors were found guilty and sentenced to jail. The case went on appeal, and in 1994 the Court of Appeal ruled that the judge had directed the jury in error, leading to the convictions being quashed.

Ultimately, the final use of the capacitors was not known. It could have been a weapon, a research project, or an entirely different civilian application. A report from an inquiry into this, the Supergun affair and other cases would go on to highlight a trend of what seemed to be overzealous, politically-driven prosecutions.

What I found most troubling was how easy it was for the Crown to argue that there was no civilian use for the capacitors, despite knowing that a university research lab had a drawer full of them. It is another example like the one cited in an earlier chapter of the man who made small timer devices for army field training and ended up spending years in jail on IRA terrorism-related offences despite a lack of proof. The political will to make examples out of people and/or countries creates bias which can steamroller over contradictory evidence—including fundamental facts.

If you think this only applies to terrorism and nuclear bombs, it doesn't. Any high-profile case can suffer misdirection due to adverse motivation in the name of justice. When the will of the government or the public is stacked against you, getting a fair trial is much harder—and that's in the UK. In the US, the same issues exist, albeit without a key safety feature: there is no significant legal aid for defence experts.

In the 1990s, Rodney Reed, a Texan man on death row, had his execution halted due to public pressure. He had been found guilty of the abduction, rape, and murder of Stacey Stites in 1996, which he denied having committed. Of the forensic evidence, DNA matching Reed was found on Stites, but the pair were in a relationship and Reed claimed they had had consensual sex the day before.

Critically, the case rested on the fact that three intact sperm cells were found in Stites' vaginal tract. Forensic experts, including one Dr. Roberto Bayardo, said in testimony that this was evidence of recent sexual activity within hours of her death.[8]

Reed's case went to trial in 1998. At that time, I was living in the US and working for the Massachusetts State Police Crime Laboratory, looking at sexual assault and murder cases.

Even in 1998, I could have told you that finding three sperm cells on a vaginal swab is entirely consistent with a claim of having had sexual intercourse the day before, and arguably inconsistent with it being more recent than that. Not only was there a list of reference papers on the subject, but the state lab ran training courses and validation checks continuously, and was always looking for willing volunteers to provide swabs from intimate areas taken hours or days after intercourse to check sperm numbers and run DNA extractions. The lab had a 'box of shame' hanging in the corridor with a list of samples the team was looking for, such as "vaginal intercourse, vaginal swabbing taken 24 hours later." Over a number of days, the list would be crossed off as staff anonymously dropped samples into the box using standard kits. (The requests for "anal intercourse" samples tended to be the hardest to fulfil, but eventually someone would do what was needed in the name of science.)

---

[8] 'Rodney Reed Files for Clemency Amidst New Affidavit Revealing Jimmy Fennell's Murder Confession', *The Innocence Project* (30 October 2019). Available at https://www.innocenceproject.org/rodney-reed-files-for-clemency-amidst-new-affidavit-revealing-jimmy-fennells-murder-confession/.

How could such a basic scientific error have happened in Reed's case? The mistake was so glaring that any competent expert should have spotted it. Had Legal Aid been available for defence experts at the time, the defence team would have had someone check it.

The US legal system, however, has a massive failing in terms of support for the defence. Defendants are entitled to legal representation, but that's it. By comparison, the District Attorney (DA) can take 12 months and throw US$100,000 worth of scientific testing at a case that a defendant can't afford to rebut.

The cases we come across in the UK tend to have gone down the wrong track due to cognitive bias and context. The same problems exist in the US, but unless you can afford proper counsel—or, as Rodney Reed did, spend 21 years in jail before the Innocence Project came on board to revisit his case—then what hope do innocent people who have been wrongly charged or convicted have?

The World Justice Project 2019 scored the US a dismal 0.37 out of 1 on whether their criminal justice system was impartial. The UK's score was 0.62.[9] A rudimentary estimate, based on extrapolating the number of known cases where further forensic work exonerated the suspect over the entire prison population, puts the proportion of innocent people in jail in the US at 1%.[10]

Whether the actual figure is 1%, lower, or higher is speculative, but it's inevitable that the justice system will put innocent people in jail from time to time, in the same way as those who commit crimes are found not guilty and set free. No matter how much money is spent on aeroplanes, they will still crash. There comes a point when you have to draw the line and say, "We've done enough."

---

[9] 'Entries for the United Kingdom and the United States in the Rule of Law Index', *World Justice Project* (2020) (accessed January 2021). Available at https://worldjusticeproject.org/rule-of-law-index/country/2020/United%20Kingdom/Criminal%20Justice/ and https://worldjustice project.org/rule-of-law-index/country/2020/United%20States/Criminal%20Justice/.

[10] 'How Many Innocent People Are in Prison?', *The Innocence Project* (12 December 2011). Available at https://www.innocenceproject.org/how-many-innocent-people-are-in-prison/.

Any risk-based system involves making a cost-benefit assessment of how much money should be spent on making said system as robust as it can be before the benefits are outstripped by the costs. In the UK, we have a (diminishing) Legal Aid budget for defence experts to mitigate the risk of the court being blinded by misunderstood or incorrect forensic science. The question for the US, then, is how much they are willing to spend to save another innocent person from jail. Perhaps 'friendly fire' could be said to be inevitable, but if it was your family member heading to jail for something you know they didn't do, would you say the same?

Civil Litigation and
Other Animals

I am a firm believer in the connectivity of things. Not in an 'Internet of Things' way, but in how life and all its actions and accessories are somehow connected via multiple different paths. Some of these connective paths are chains, which makes them easier to understand, but some are huge, undulating grids with spurs and intersecting chains from other sources which are so complex that deciphering the connections becomes humanly impossible.

Connections affect all of us. We might look at our most profound moments in life and realise they are a result of a series of events which can be traced back to a particular point in time. For me, living in the US can be traced back nine years before the move to a man named Martin, whom I met on my first day at the University of Hull. I went to the University of Hull because Sheila, who lived three doors down from my parents' house, also went to Hull, and hired the disco that I DJ'ed for to hold an event when I was 17. The trail is easy to spot with the benefit of hindsight.

Criminal investigations enjoy no such benefit. Trying to put together a series of events to elucidate evidence, sometimes over and over again, is a painstaking process with many dead ends and false leads.

The process is no different in the world of health and safety. For every injury or loss, there are normally a number of factors and/or events which cascade into each other to result in an accident.

Let's say someone trips over a power cord lying across a corridor at work, and they fall and break their shoulder. The incident is quite specific: there's a power cord on the floor and someone tripped over it. However, a number of factors which led to the cord being put there form a chain leading up to that point, such as:

- There was no power in the office which the cord led to, as the socket broke three months ago.

- The broken socket was reported to maintenance four times, but nothing was done.

- The cord had been used every day since and no one said not to use it.

- The manager walked by it every day and didn't say anything.

- Three months went by with no accidents.

- A number of people also tripped over the cord, but did not say anything or report it.

- No one put a cover over the cord or ran the cord above the corridor instead.

- Health and safety training did not include being aware of trip hazards.

The factors form a kind of domino chain leading up to the accident in that if one of them had been addressed, the chain would have been broken, and the accident would not have happened. This is why risk assessments result in accident prevention.

Steps which remove these dangerous 'dominos' are enforced through health and safety laws and regulations, coupled with good practice and good management. For example, both the UK and US legally require employers to take steps to ensure the safety and health of their employees as far as is reasonably practicable.[1] If you work as a forensic scientist,

---

[1] Health and Safety at Work etc. Act 1974 (UK) and Occupational Safety and Health Act (OSH Act of 1970) (US). Available at https://www.legislation.gov.uk/ukpga/1974/37/contents and https://www.osha.gov/laws-regs/oshact/completeoshact.

your employer should provide you with protective gear to stop you from being exposed to bloodborne viruses or bacteria at a crime scene. They should also train you how to use the gear correctly and safely, and you, the employee, are required to follow the guidance on how to wear it.

If this is done, then even if you're dealing with a putrefying, semi-liquid body lying in a shallow grave in the woods in the rain, then you should be protected from most risks—unless, as happened to a friend of mine, you slip and fall on top of the corpse (in which case, you would hope a written plan exists for addressing such contingencies).

In the above example, all measures were taken to protect the individual, but the scene was outdoors and it was raining. In most cases, the boots which we were required to wear at crime scenes would have provided decent protection, but they became slippery in the rain. A change in conditions meant the regular protective equipment had actually become dangerous. So employers and employees not only have a responsibility to provide and use safety equipment; there must be a dynamic component to allow for change as well.

What is interesting about the above example is that the boots which are normally worn to a crime scene become notoriously slippery in liquid, like water or blood. I once almost landed face down in a pool of blood that had gathered in a doorway; I'd figured I'd be able to hop over it, but landed with one foot in the blood, which caused me to skid forward. If not for a quick and thankfully accurate grab of the door frame, I'd have gone down. All that protective gear will only go so far. After all, it's not a space suit.

The point is that slippery boots are a well-known problem; my slip in blood—thankfully without a major accident—is what's known as a 'near miss'. Getting a tingle from touching a broken plug is a near miss. If you leave a power cord on the floor and someone trips on it but doesn't fall, that's a near miss. What happens with near misses is that, at some point, they end in major injuries. This is why employers like to hear about near misses: it gives them a chance to remove a 'domino' to block any domino effect that could have led to a serious incident.

There is, however, a difference between the cause of an accident and the cause of a loss. They are investigated in the same way, but the connections and paths leading up to each may be different.

Take the Nottingham Railway Station fire, which started in a recently remodelled public bathroom in the early hours of 12 January 2018. Between physical and business losses, the fire caused an estimated £5.6 million in damage.[2]

The fire was started by a drug addict called Gemma, who pled guilty to starting it and was sentenced to 25 months in jail for arson. That might seem like a light sentence, but if you separate the cause of the *fire* and the cause of the *losses*, there are two different things going on.

There is a reasonably foreseeable risk that, at some point, someone will—either accidentally or on purpose—set fire to a public toilet. As such, it is critical that any remodellings take this into account. That wasn't done in the Nottingham fire; deficiencies and apparent short-cuts in the remodelling of the bathrooms allowed the fire to spread beyond the toilet block and through the station, causing a complete shutdown.

The Crown's case also didn't consider the long delay before staff reported the fire to the emergency services. Had the fire been reported as soon as it was discovered, it might not have spread so far.

These issues shifted scrutiny of the fire away from Gemma and towards the designers, builders, architects, and inspectors, as well as the staff's training in fire-preparedness. All these potentially shared the burden for the fire as contributory dominos in the chain.

This is the cornerstone of civil litigation: blame enters the picture if it can be argued that had a piece *not* been there, an injury or loss could have been avoided. And 'where there's blame, there's a claim'.

---

[2] R. Sherdley, 'Nottingham Railway Station Fire was an 'Accident Waiting to Happen,' Court Told', *Nottinghamshire Live* (13 August 2019). Available at https://www.nottinghampost.com/news/local-news/nottingham-railway-station-fire-accident-3206532.

The expression dates back to an article from 2001, in which the author, David Budworth, gave advice on how to make claims against insurance companies.[3] The year before, *The Guardian* ran an article titled "It wasn't my fault" on the shifting culture of blame and rising compensation in the UK.[4] "Does this really mean that we're moving towards a more American style of trigger-happy litigation, where you sue first and ask questions later?" it asked. (British perceptions of US civil litigation are such that Americans will sue for pretty much anything.)

The UK, or at least England and Wales, has an unusual history in terms of civil claims. When I started my career in 1991, civil claims were infrequent and settlement amounts were modest. The idea that legal costs could be met through contingency fees (i.e. the 'no win, no fee' model) was regularly decried. Richard Abel, quoting an article from *The Times*, said that contingency fees allowed solicitors to tout for cases by "haunting the side doors of [our] large metropolitan hospitals."[5]

The UK's opposition to contingency fees continued through the decades, looking at the US' experience in a decidedly negative light. In a 1989 Green Paper on the future of the legal profession, Lord Mackay of Clashfern was quoted as saying:

> "...[E]xperience in the USA suggests that contingency fees i) encourage juries to award excessive damages; and ii) encourage litigants to proceed with cases with very little merit, leading to an explosion of litigation."[6]

---

[3] D. Budworth, 'Where There's Blame There's a Claim', *This is MONEY* (12 January 2001). Available at https://www.thisismoney.co.uk/money/mortgageshome/article-1560852/Where-theres-blame-theres-a-claim.html.

[4] S. Coughlan, 'It Wasn't My Fault', *The Guardian* (7 October 2000). Available at https://www.theguardian.com/money/2000/oct/07/1.

[5] R. Abel, 'An American Hamburger Stand in St. Paul's Cathedral: Replacing Legal Aid with Conditional Fees in English Personal Injury Litigation', *DePaul Law Review* 51(2) (2001). Available at https://via.library.depaul.edu/law-review/vol51/iss2/6.

[6] Lord Mackay of Clashfern, *Green Paper on the Legal Profession*, UK Parliament (17 January 1989). Available at https://api.parliament.uk/historic-hansard/written-answers/1989/jan/25/legal-profession-green-paper.

He further noted that "United States society is litigious on a scale not known in England and Wales," adding that their system "encourages 'bounty-hunting' by US lawyers."

Perhaps the most unusual feature of UK civil litigation in its earlier years was that Legal Aid was available to poorer members of the public, giving them fair redress in pursuing a claim. In other words, the government would help people pursue a legitimate civil claim for damages if they couldn't afford it. This notion was very foreign to the US, where one commentator suggested that "the English Bar was propelled into becoming a handmaiden of the Welfare State."[7] The President of the American Bar Association (ABA) went so far as to cite the UK model for Legal Aid as the greatest threat to the American legal profession, aside from the infiltration of Communism.[8]

When I started working in forensics in 1991, we encountered a number of civil claims which were supported by Legal Aid. This continued until around 1999, when reforms to Legal Aid put an end to things.

In the years following this, there was an initial lull, but then came the advertisements, followed by the cold calls which boldly stated, "We heard you had an accident recently that was not your fault...," and ultimately the text messages repeating much the same. 'Claim' culture—the mirror of 'blame' culture—has grown rapidly in recent years, especially in road traffic cases, where claims doubled between 2004–2013.[9] It apparently took a few years after the switch to a contingency fee system for solicitors to catch up and start to market a service more like the US model.

---

[7]   K. Hughes, 'The Contingent Fee Contract in Massachusetts', *Boston Uni Law Review* XLIII(1) 1–19 (1963). Available at https://www.repository.law.indiana.edu/facpub/1999/.

[8]   R. Storey, 'The Legal Profession versus Regimentation: A Program to Counter Socialization', *American Bar Association Journal* 37(2) 100–103, 167–168 (1951). Available at https://www.jstor.org/stable/25717542.

[9]   R. Lewis, 'Compensation Culture Reviewed: Incentives to Claim and Damage Levels', *Journal of Personal Injury Law* 4 209–225 (2014). Available at https://doi.org/10.2139/ssrn.2467110.

In the US, civil litigation mostly operates on a contingency fee basis, and it's fair to say that the lawyers involved in it range from those advertising professional services in a professional manner to virtual ambulance-chasers. While driving across Alligator Alley, Florida, in December 2019, I discovered radio channel 102.7, known as 'The Beach'—only it didn't say that on the car radio. Despite technology allowing the song title and artist's name to be displayed while a song is playing, the station actually showed the phone number and name of Anidjar & Levine Accident Lawyers.

You might expect the 'no win, no fee' model to result in poor practices and opportunistic lawyers. In one historical case from 1821, a New York litigant ended up paying his lawyer a fee that was 94% of the value of the estate that he won.[10] However, a 1992 review from Dana and Spier found that contingency fees generally ranged between 25–50%, and such arrangements tended to weed out frivolous and nuisance lawsuits.[11]

When it comes to forensic science, similar concerns—valid or not—over unscrupulous behaviour exist regarding 'pay to say' expert witnesses.

In the UK, Legal Aid-funded criminal defence work pays around £72–£90 (US$95–$120) an hour, while charges for civil work are in the range of £200–£225 (US$260–$330) an hour. In the US, expert fees for civil work tend to be around £375 (US$500) an hour. Given this, it's easy to see why experts might want to keep clients happy and cases alive with a stream of research, reports, follow-up reports and depositions. With such high fees, would a jury perceive an expert to be truly independent or a hired gun?

---

[10] P. Karsten, 'Enabling the Poor to Have Their Day in Court: The Sanctioning of Contingency Fee Contracts, a History to 1940', *DePaul Law Review* 47(2) (1998). Available at https://via.library.depaul.edu/law review/vol47/iss2/3/.

[11] J.D. Dana and K.E. Spier, 'Expertise and Contingent Fees: The Role of Asymmetric Information in Attorney Compensation', *Harvard Law School Discussion Paper 110 5/92* (1992). Available at http://www.law.harvard.edu/programs/olin_center/papers/pdf/Spier_110.pdf.

Herein lies the problem for forensic experts who work under a contingency fee system. Your client, a lawyer, works in an adversarial system where getting paid, to some degree, relies on them winning. Future clients will come back to you depending on how well you perform. This gives rise to the temptation to maintain a relationship by pushing a matter as far as you can in your client's favour, while leading counsel to believe their case is stronger than it really is. And since most cases settle before trial, the truth of that precarious position rarely comes out. Even if the opposing expert disagrees, the lawyers will put this down to dishonesty of the other expert and not their own.

This is where two significant differences regarding forensic experts emerge between the US and the UK.

The first is that in England and Wales, the criminal, civil, and family courts all take the independence of forensic experts quite literally: experts are under an overriding duty to the court and not the side they are being paid by.[12] As a result, in cases of differing expert opinions, the judge will normally ask the experts to meet and go over the points in contention, and come up with a schedule of agreed and disagreed points and the reasons for disagreement. This is often a short summary, no more than a few pages long, although I've seen experts misunderstand this and essentially reproduce their entire report under a different header. These are the experts who, despite having made a lot of money out of being an expert witness, haven't given evidence in court.

The second is that the US has a concept called 'spoliation of evidence', which falls under Rule 37 of the Federal Rules of Civil Procedure.[13] This is where evidence that can be reasonably expected to be relevant to a case has been altered or destroyed due to negligence or intent. If a company which sent out an email admitting to an issue deletes that email, that's spoliation. If the court accepts spoliation occurred, it can

---

[12] See Part 35.3 of the Civil Procedure Rules 1998, Part 19.2 of the Criminal Procedure Rules 2020, and Part 25.3 of the Family Procedure Rules 2010.

[13] See Rule 37 of the Federal Rules of Civil Procedure.

impose sanctions, which include restriction of evidence and punitive damages.

As a result, the US is far more conscientious about not getting rid of evidence than the UK. In the UK, if I ask to see an item in a case that is critical to the outcome, only to find that it was thrown away, I can expect a collective shrug and a muted apology. In the US, there would be fire and brimstone, not to mention legal and financial consequences.

However, with the rise of contingency fees, what I've seen in both the US and the UK are plaintiffs who believe they are due a payout, and experts who walk a fine line between what they know to be the reality of the evidence and what the client would rather hear.

The value of the system in England and Wales is that mechanisms exist to expose experts who sail too close to the wind. In one case, the medical expert and forensic chemist for the plaintiff, Mr. Smith, both opined that he had been exposed to hydrogen sulphide gas as a result of his working conditions and the high winds that day. The funny thing about that case was that the only person who mentioned the windy weather was Mr. Smith. The two 'independent' experts acting for him had formed critical opinions on this matter without checking the weather. It turned out that on the day of the incident, there was barely a gust of wind.

The more probable reason for Mr. Smith's injury was that he hadn't worn a mask, as was required by health and safety regulations. This point had been ignored by his experts despite their legal duty to tell the court the whole truth. The court ordered the forensic experts for both the plaintiff and defendant to meet and produce a joint schedule of points they agreed or disagreed on, which is done strictly between the experts and without any legal interference or presence. The plaintiff's forensic chemist conceded the points about the weather and Mr. Smith's failure to wear a mask, and a settlement was reached.

In another case in the US, a fire gutted a second-floor condo in a two-storey building with a typical wooden structure. The occupant had no insurance cover. The fire patterns demonstrated a heavy area of burning on the floor, around an area where a thin two-pin extension cord had run under a sofa and to an electric heater, with a three-pin plug that had been adapted to make it fit. The cord had not been designed to take this kind of power, and overheating of the cord was a likely explanation for the fire—but if it were true, nobody could be sued.

Instead, the fire expert for the plaintiff claimed the fire had originated in a computer monitor made by a well-known manufacturer. The monitor had been atop a table on one side of the room. The fire damage alone showed the fire couldn't have started in that area, but the litigation continued for several years, involving more experts in electronics and engineering.

The plaintiff's expert remained convinced it was the monitor. He produced an X-ray of the transformer from inside the monitor showing a dark spot on the image, which he opined was the cause of the breakdown that led to the fire. An electrical expert for the defendant said it was nonsense, as the transformer contained a ceramic-encased fuse; in his opinion, the dark spot was the gap created by the body of the fuse, which didn't show up on the X-ray.

As a result of the disagreement, three experts, along with their legal representatives, attended a facility to see the transformer being pulled apart. Some had to fly to get there. Over several hours, the burned and melted debris was slowly removed layer by layer, revealing the transformer's insides. With each layer, the transformer became cleaner and shinier until a ball of gleaming copper was left. There was no fire damage at all: the transformer had been cooked from the outside, not the inside. Even with this overwhelming evidence, the plaintiff's expert wouldn't budge, and the case went to arbitration.

Despite its frustrations, civil work does have its advantages. It pays double or even triple per hour, compared to what the same expert would be paid by Legal Aid. The reports tend to be more involved and have more value, and there are often follow-up reports, meetings and questions to answer—especially if, like the expert above, you keep spinning the story. At the end of the day, experts hardly ever have to go to court, which means the ones who sail close to the wind (or even straight into it) are never exposed on cross-examination as the charlatans they really are.

There are other critical advantages of working outside the criminal arena. One is that you tend to have much more time and resources. Unlike the sad situation in the criminal justice system in England and Wales, where forensic evidence is often reviewed a week before a trial (and sometimes even after the trial has started), in civil matters, there may be months, if not years, to get all the facts straight and produce a report.

In major cases, civil parties often enjoy access to resources that the police often don't have. In the US, with their laws on spoliation, the police and concerned parties like insurance companies tend to work in tandem to ensure all available resources are exhausted. In a complex building collapse case, they might bring in cranes and lifting equipment to slowly take the structure apart while safely allowing the next stage of work to continue. In the UK, it's more likely that work would be halted, with further investigation precluded due to structural instability.

In fairness, it's not like public and insurance mutual assistance never happens in the UK. A massive explosion in Liverpool once took out a town block and injured 81 people; the investigation was multi-handed, involving resources supplied by various private and public groups, and was done over several days. However, this is more the exception than the norm. (In this case, the findings led to the prosecution of both a furniture shop owner—for deliberately uncapping a gas pipe and turning it on—and the gas company for failing to isolate the pipe.)[14]

The first civil fire case I worked on in the US took place in 1994, while I was walking to work in Cambridge, Massachusetts. At the time, I had

[14] 'New Ferry Gas Explosion Was 'Insurance Job Gone Wrong'", *BBC News* (9 January 2019) and L. Traynor, 'Gas Company Fined £350,000 for Their Part in Devasting New Ferry Explosion', *Liverpool Echo* (14 October 2019). Available at https://www.bbc.com/news/uk-england-merseyside-46814237 and https://www.liverpoolecho.co.uk/news/liverpool-news/gas-company-fined-350000-part-15734063.

moved to Massachusetts, gotten married, and was living in a spacious one-bedroom apartment on Charles Street in Beacon Hill. Work was a walk across the 'salt and pepper' bridge which spanned the Charles River, linking Boston to Cambridge.

It was a gloriously warm June day with blue skies. Halfway across the bridge, I noticed a faint odour of wood smoke. I turned around and on the horizon to the north of the Boston skyline was a massive plume of brown and black smoke. Something big was on fire.

The Rapids Furniture warehouse on the Charlestown waterfront was aflame, and the blaze took 200 firefighters to extinguish. Lt. Stephen Minehan went in to help rescue several firefighters who had gone missing inside the sprawling warehouse.[15] The others made it out, but tragically, the act cost the Lieutenant his life.

Witnesses claimed to have seen what they thought was a boat on fire underneath a section of the warehouse that sat on pilings over the Charles River estuary.[16] A few weeks later, I found myself employed as a fire investigator at a company called FirePro, sitting in a rented boat bobbing up and down underneath the burned remains of the warehouse.

Working with FirePro took me all over the eastern half of the US, often at short notice. We'd get a call to attend a fire, and within two days I would be on a flight armed only with a video recorder, camera, Dictaphone, and some scene basics such as a hard hat, gloves and a tape measure. Once I'd picked up my rental car at the airport, I'd drive to a hardware store and buy a shovel, trowel, bucket, and other things I might need before heading off, often into the wilds of nowhere, to locate the scene and talk to the local fire department.

---

[15] See the 'Fatality Notice for Lt. Stephen F. Minehan', *US Fire Administration* (13 June 2012). Available at https://apps.usfa.fema.gov/firefighter-fatalities/fatalityData/detail?fatalityId=627.

[16] 'Boston Fire Lt. Dies Saving Others', *United Press International Online Archives* (24 June 1994). Available at https://www.upi.com/Archives/1994/06/24/Boston-fire-Lt-dies-saving-others/7782772430400/.

In mid-July 1994, I landed in Ohio to investigate a mobile home that had caught fire a week earlier, outside a small town near the West Virginia border. It was dark by the time I got the rental car, and I drove east into the countryside until I realised I could see flashes of light in my peripheral vision. I finally pulled over next to the pitch-black woodland, wondering if I was imagining things, only to see more flashes in the dark. Fireflies: I'd never seen them before.

The next day, I went to the county Chamber of Commerce to get a map of the area. The young man behind the counter was tall and heavy-set. He asked where I was headed to, so I gave him the street name and he nodded.

"You're here about the fire then?" he asked.

"Ye-es," I replied cautiously. "That was quick," he replied, and showed me how to get there. It turned out he was a volunteer firefighter who had attended the fire.

After driving for 30 minutes, I finally wound up on a long road, dotted sporadically with homes on large lots and a lot of scrubby woodland with some open enclosures for animals on one side. On the opposite side of the road was farmland. Noting the numbers on the mailboxes, I eventually stopped outside a ranch-style home set well back from the road, with a burned-out mobile home sitting on the driveway. This was the place.

A heavy-duty pickup truck with 'Fire' on the sides was already parked outside. The man who got out was in his 40s and of medium height, with brown hair, large glasses and a thick moustache. He seemed cautious.

"I'm the Deputy Fire Chief," he said.

"Nice to meet you. How do you know I was here?" I asked.

"Chamber of Commerce called and said you were coming," he said, and paused to consider his next words. "I came by as you just don't walk up and knock on someone's front door here; they might just shoot you."

Perplexed, I asked him how one ought to go about knocking in that case. He shrugged his shoulders and said, "You stand at the gate and holler."

I'd only been in the US a year at the time, and was starting to realise how little I knew of anything outside of the Boston bubble I lived in. We chatted for a while before he commented, "You got here quick, the Fire Marshall's not even been."

I figured a week wasn't exactly jumping out of the starting gate, so I ventured to ask why it had taken the Fire Marshall a week to get there.

"Aw shit, you're here for the fire last week!" he exclaimed with a laugh. "There was another one last night. Same trailer. They musta' heard you were coming!"

The ability of US state officials, insurance companies and/or manufacturer's representatives to work together cannot be understated. This not only allows for pooling of massive resources in criminal matters, but in civil cases where a duty of care to the public comes in, it allows for multiple sets of eyes and opinions to assess everything first-hand. The outcome can then be reported back into the Consumer Product Safety Commission (CPSC), whose mandate is to protect the public from unreasonable risks of injury or death associated with the use of consumer products.

The CPSC estimates that consumer product incidents cost the US around US$1 trillion a year.[17] The sheer amount of money tied up in civil litigation surrounding such incidents may well have driven the need for a bureau like the CPSC.

Such a system, however, barely exists in the UK, despite complaints about the lack of centralised reporting to help push manufacturers to

---

[17] See the CPSC website at https://www.cpsc.gov/node/12696.

recall dangerous items.[18] I've no doubt that some tragedies in the UK could have been avoided with a better reporting system.

In the UK, there was a significant delay before Hotpoint, an appliance manufacturer, finally recalled several items which were known to be defective—by which time a significant number of catastrophic fires had occurred.[19]

---

[18] L.F. Wood, 'UK Consumer Product Recall Review: The Government Response to the Independent Recall Review', *Department for Business, Innovation & Skills* BIS/16/69 (February 2016). Available at https://assets.publishing.service.gov.uk/government/uploads/system/uploads/attachment_data/file/500422/bis-16-69-consumer-product-recall-government-response.pdf.

[19] 'Man Describes How His Hotpoint Dishwasher Caught Fire', *ITV News* (23 April 2013). Available at https://www.itv.com/news/2013-04-23/man-describes-how-his-hotpoint-dishwasher-caught-fire/.

The 1990s Crime Lab

It's funny how things in life work out. When I first moved to the US, I spent considerable effort trying to get a job in either fire investigation or at a crime lab (at which time there were two: Boston City and the Massachusetts State Police).

I sent my CVs out and made follow-up calls every month or so. After a few months, Larry, who worked in Human Resources with the State of Massachusetts office, came to recognise my voice. As soon as he heard me on the phone he would boom, "Dr. Schudel!" and then proceed to tell me there were no vacancies. This went on until I eventually landed a role with FirePro.

Around two years in, I realised that fire investigation work was waning at the firm, and nothing seemed to be bumping it up. Sensing something had to give, I made my excuses one Friday afternoon and left the office around 3:00PM, specifically so I could get home and give Larry a call. (It might seem odd to go to such lengths in this day and age, but back then mobile phones were a commodity for the rich, drug dealers, or rich drug dealers. I couldn't call from work, and the only other option was to use the phone at home.)

I picked up the phone and called the same State number, wondering who would answer. "Dr. Schudel!" boomed Larry at the other end, "How've ya been?"

We chatted briefly. "Funny you should call," he said. "We have five vacancies at the lab, and the deadline is 5:00PM today."

It took me a moment to process. "5:00PM today?" I replied incredulously.

"Yes sir. I don't care what you get to me: letter, fax, CV, whatever, but it needs to be in by 5:00PM."

By 4:50PM I'd faxed a letter with my CV from a friend's workplace and called to make sure Larry had it. I was in the pot.

It took a few months, but I eventually landed a job as a Forensic Chemist at the Massachusetts State Police Crime Laboratory and started my training as a Criminalist. I had finally turned away from the dark side.

One of the core differences in forensics between the UK and the US is the role of criminalists. In the UK, the different laboratory roles are broken down across various sections. Taking a T-shirt from a murder victim as an example, a biologist would be looking at blood, while a chemist would be looking for fibres and other materials.

In the US, the criminalist was the 'jack of all trades'; they would look for everything on the item, including isolating and confirming the presence of human blood or semen, and then send any findings on for analysis in the different specialisms as needed.

The other difference was scene work. In the UK, crime scene investigators (CSIs) handle pretty much every scene, no matter how complex. If you worked in a forensic lab, that's where you remained. In the US, lab chemists would be called out to many major incidents, especially if there was blood or semen to look for. In short, the police would take their own photographs and fingerprints, and then you, the forensic scientist, would collect your own evidence, bring it back to the lab and analyse it, possibly as soon as the next day if the matter was urgent.

Excited, anxious, and bright-eyed, I embarked on a new and dynamic career. What I'd forgotten was that this was government work, which also meant unions, timekeeping, people who clearly had no fear of being fired no matter what they did, and others with no concern for customer service. In other words, it was a bit like walking into any government or council-run organisation to get anything done in the days before the internet. While cases of bad behaviour are normally managed in private firms, as they directly affect revenue one way or another, at the state government level, they just fester away.

Don't get me wrong: most of the forensic scientists were talented and driven. There were those who put in 150%. But the phrase 'a bad apple spoils the barrel' was never more apt, as demonstrated by the Annie Dookhan scandal discussed in an earlier chapter.

For me, the greatest and most appalling problem with the Massachusetts State lab was actually common to many state, county, and city labs throughout the US. It was something borne out of archaic methods, developed at a time when life was a whole lot simpler: the backlog.

When I started at the lab in 1998, there were around 2,000 sexual assault cases in backlog, by which I mean there were literally 2,000 cases sitting on a shelf in the giant walk-in fridge. Yes, 2,000. Even when I started on casework, my daily pile of cases grew by the week without any kind of prioritisation. Each week, another stack of beige folders would be plopped onto the existing ones assigned to me. The only person doing any kind of priority assessment on them was me. And I hated it.

Each beige folder contained a case outline, a short summary of the issues and the evidence submitted. Take these two example cases in the pile:

- A 19-year-old woman got drunk at her first semester in college and woke up in a bed to find a male student having sex with her.

- A 27-year-old woman left for work at 7:30AM and was abducted at her front door. Her captor forced her to drive to an ATM to withdraw money, then another 20 miles to a field where she was raped. She was then left in the field while her attacker drove off in her car.

The decision to put the college case further down the pile fell to me. Each week, my list grew with cases that I could never complete. Some involved violent rapes, children, or vulnerable adults. Each week, the pile grew, and each week I had to decide whether cases like the college one should be shuffled further down or not. It was the lab's unspoken dilemma.

In 2020, a roundtable discussion with the US Department of Justice (DoJ) highlighted:

> "Advocates cautioned against widespread misconceptions about acquaintance rape, noting that the majority of sexual assaults are committed by someone the victim knows. Treating acquaintance rape as 'less serious' than rape by a stranger will only hinder efforts to eliminate the backlog."[1]

I couldn't agree more. It bothers me to this day that I had to decide which case came next, without any guidance or process, while the system and protocols in place at the lab were as unbending as they were foolishly dogmatic, and the backlog remained as bad as ever. 'First one in is the next one out' simply wouldn't work when there were cases in the walk-in fridge that had been there for years.

At the time, the state's answer was to allow one day of overtime per week to try and catch up with the backlog. But with the number of cases per month continuing to increase anyway, the extra day made no difference.

One main issue with the backlog was the procedure regarding microscopy. In a typical sexual assault case, vaginal swabs would be taken from the complainant and smeared onto two glass slides. Both the swabs and slides would be dried and packaged into a swab box and slide holder respectively. These were placed in a sexual assault evidence collection (SAEC) kit and sent to the lab along with other swabs, slides, hair combings, underwear and any other relevant items.

The lab's method was to stain the slide first to look for any sperm cells. If you found at least one sperm cell (preferably more), you rated the slide depending on the number of cells and submitted the case for DNA profiling. If not, you took one of the swabs, checked it for

---

[1] Department of Justice, *Summary of Proceedings Eliminating the Rape Kit Backlog: A Roundtable to Explore a Victim-centered Approach* (Washington D.C., 11–12 May 2010).

acid phosphatase (AP), cut out a small piece, centrifuged it in saline and then made your own slide to stain and look for cells. If no sperm cells were found and the AP was negative, then it was a negative finding.

It sounds straightforward, except that if you're looking for sperm cells under a 1,000x microscope, a standard 75mm x 25mm slide smeared across much of its area is like looking for small glass marbles on a football pitch. It's fine if there's 10,000 of them; but if there's one or two, let alone zero, you can sit there for a whole day searching for either very little or nothing at all.

The rationale for this approach was to make sure that, in cases where there were only a few sperm cells, you avoided cutting the original swab and thus minimised the risk of destroying already very low levels of sperm DNA. However, the problem with this was that cases with only a few sperm cells in them were relatively rare, and negative cases relatively common. In rape cases, it wasn't unusual for the suspect to either use a condom, ejaculate elsewhere, or be unable to ejaculate at all. This meant that the 2,000 case backlog had largely been amassed due to the pursuit of negative cases.

One solution would have been to put a time limit on examining slides, such as 15 minutes (i.e. to move on to the swabs if you didn't find sperm cells in that time). But this wasn't adopted, and the backlog kept growing.

The Massachusetts State lab wasn't alone in this. A census of public forensic labs in the US found that at the end of 2002, there was a backlog of 262,637 cases across all labs and all submissions (including drugs). This was ~10% of the submissions,[2] of which 49,000 were for DNA. A 2004 report published by Washington State University under a DoJ

---

[2] US Department of Justice, 'Census of Publicly Funded Forensic Crime Laboratories 2002' (NCJ Document 207205), *Bureau of Justice Statistics Bulletin* (February 2005). Available at https://bjs.ojp.gov/content/pub/pdf/cpffcl02.pdf.

award estimated there was a country-wide backlog of over half a million sexual assault cases.[3]

Even today, labs are still playing catch-up to the sexual assault case backlog, as has been highlighted by advocacy groups like End the Backlog.[4] In 2019, it was reported that the governor of Austin, Texas, signed off on more legislation to end the backlog of rape test kits.[5]

But that's now, and this was over 20 years ago. Trying to decide the fate of people I didn't know based on a snapshot contained in a beige folder seemed harsh and unnerving. I knew that a portion of the cases would never see a courtroom, but that shouldn't have been my choice to make. They should all have been processed in a timely fashion, and that could only have come through systemic change—which only happened long after I had left the lab.

Amongst the cases I worked on, there were a few that stood out. A 12-year-old reported that she fell unconscious after someone put a cloth over her mouth, and later woke up bleeding heavily from the vagina. She ran to a neighbour for help, who called emergency services. When the beige folder containing the sexual assault evidence kit from her case landed in my inbox, it didn't take any consideration; I got on with the job that day.

I did the usual, which was to remove the vaginal smear slides and stain them with haematoxylin and eosin. When I mounted and magnified them, I saw something I hadn't seen before: the slide was covered in cells of unearthly-looking size and quantity, which were roundish and

---

[3]   N.P. Lovrich et al., *National Forensic DNA Study Report* (NCJ Document 203970), Office of Justice Programs, US Department of Justice (December 2003). Available at https://www.ojp.gov/ncjrs/virtual-library/abstracts/national-forensic-dna-study-report.

[4]   See *End the Backlog*. Available at http://www.endthebacklog.org/backlog/what-rape-kit-backlog.

[5]   F. Cantú, 'Governor Signs HB 8 into Law to End Backlog of Rape Test Kits in Sex Assault Cases', *CBS Austin* (5 June 2019). Available at https://cbsaustin.com/news/local/governor-signs-hb-8-into-law-to-end-backlog-of-rape-test-kits-in-sex-assault-cases.

faintly stained. I moved the slide around, trying another quadrant, and it was the same.

Shaking my head, I asked a colleague to have a look. "No idea," he said. "Bacteria, maybe?"

I laughed. If bacteria were that big, I explained, we'd never get out the door. "Well," he continued, matter-of-fact, "it's not sperm, so move on."

In a way, this was symptomatic of the dogma that tends to plague forensic science to this day. ISO 17025 requires specific methods to be followed, and the groups which enforce this are ever-ready to slam down on those who stray from the path with an almighty hand. People are scared to go outside any box other than the one they're supposed to tick.

But I couldn't let it slide. Something deep in my mind told me I had seen this before. I checked around the small but well-stocked Massachusetts Crime Lab library and pulled out a copy of the Met's lab manual, dating back to the late 1970s or 1980s. There it was: a hand-drawn black-and-white sketch of the same oddly faint cell, canine spermatozoa.

I also managed to blag a favour from a friend of a friend who was a vet. He happened to be getting a vial of dog semen that Friday to artificially inseminate a dog and spared me a few drops. I stained the sample on a slide and it was identical.

In a busy, dogmatic, and 17025-compliant lab, it would have been easy to tick the 'negative' box for sperm cells and this child's ordeal would have gone unnoticed. Testing a system is part of how a system evolves, and for a defence expert, is par for the course. Always check your sources, and never assume the status quo is right.

Once you put aside the stifling, treacle-like bureaucracy that cocooned the lab, there was a sense of camaraderie and teamwork that kept the place driven. I worked the evening shift, so dinner break meant going out for Chinese or Thai, or having pizza in front of the canteen TV while watching *Buffy the Vampire Slayer*. When our shift ended, we would sometimes roll out around 11:00PM and mooch our way back to Boston for a night out.

Work was varied and often unpredictable. I once ended up in a barn in sleepy town a two-hour drive west, looking for sperm on a sofa from an alleged sexual assault weeks before. It was so hot that day that the sofa felt like it would combust if you put a light near it (but we did find sperm cells).

Two seasons later, I was standing in a freezing cold alley in Springfield, swabbing the body of a partially naked woman. She was later suspected to be one of the victims of the serial killer Alfred Gaynor.[6]

I was called one night to a shooting murder in the same town to look at a suspected blood cast-off pattern over the ceiling of a bedsit apartment. It turned out to be a suspected grease cast-off pattern from a frying pan in the kitchen. (I wonder to this day how the grease got up there; it went halfway across the room.)

One time, after a tragic hit-and-run involving a small boy, I was 'bunnied up' (wearing the white coverall suit that you often see CSIs wearing in crime TV programmes), carefully picking samples from the front of the suspect's car, while a police video camera rolled what felt like inches from my face. Afterwards, I asked the detective why they felt the need to video it. He laughed and shrugged, "We didn't need to video it. That was Fox News!"

Being part of the lab meant you were also part of the State Police, which meant you got to drive the unmarked State Police cruiser. In the words of Elwood Blues from *The Blues Brothers*, "It's got a cop motor…It's got cop tires, cop suspension, cop shocks." You put your foot down and off it went like a rocket. Any time you were on call, you had the option

---

[6] S. Reitz, 'Handyman Admits to Killing At Least 8 Mass. Women', *NBC News* (13 December 2010). Available at https://www.nbcnews.com/id/40629524.

of leaving your Honda Civic at the lab and taking the cruiser home instead.

Don't get me wrong: an unmarked State Police cruiser wasn't exactly the best CSI vehicle you could hope for. There was no storage, which meant that at any major scene, you had to ask the officer-in-charge to help get the packaged evidence back to the lab. There was no space for scene chemicals, no scene lighting, and no drawers full of supplies. It did, however, have a centre console with two cup holders, which flipped up to reveal a hidden police radio and switches for the sirens and lights. Cool.

One of those switches was very important: it toggled between a normal car horn to a police wail with flashing red and blue lights. As crime lab civilians, we weren't 'red and blue' trained, so every time we got in the vehicle, we had to check to make sure that switch was firmly set to civilian mode.

One day, I was on the I-95 South, heading towards the Route 9 intersection, when I realised I'd forgotten to check the switch mode. The freeway was always a bit crazy with impatient drivers running down the fast lane before cutting across to try to make the slipway exit, which was invariably jammed with cars from people doing just that. All this meant that traffic in the faster lanes got the overspill and suffered from sudden stationary pockets—like the one my cruiser was about to go into.

As I was slowing down, a kind gentleman cut right in front me and slammed on his brakes. The cop brakes were sharp, and having lived in Boston for a few years at this point, I was used to the driving customs. I hit the horn in response…and the entire car wailed and lit up like a red and blue Christmas tree.

In the US, police sirens behind you like that mean only one thing: "Pull over!" The driver in front slumped visibly and started to move towards the emergency lane; every car around me suddenly moved back by 100 metres, leaving me all the room I needed to follow. The trouble was, I had no right of arrest. I was a civilian. As the driver slowed into the next lane, I pulled up alongside his car, waved a stern finger at him, then sped away as if it was all planned. I imagine he thought he was the one getting a lucky break.

One early evening, we were called out to Quincy Police Department, only to find that they hadn't even exercised the search warrant but wanted us ready to go when they did. A lab colleague came with me, and we waited an hour or so at the station until we got the green light to leave. The police officer said, "Follow us,", hopped into his car, turned on his blue lights, and vanished.

Now, I've mentioned that we weren't trained in pursuit driving—but the police officer didn't know that, and he also hadn't told us the address. Off I sped like a very poor copy of Lewis Hamilton, running several stop signs and making some questionable turns. Thankfully, as it was dark outside, I managed to keep his flashing lights in sight. We followed him to a house, which was boxed in with several police vehicles when we got there.

We were asked to park a discreet distance away while the warrant was executed. You never knew if situations could turn into a gunfight. We watched as the police knocked on the door, got no reply, and forced it open. The suspect was out—but apparently not his dog.

A detective trotted across the street towards us. It was a warm night and we were outside, leaning on the car.

"You the State lab?"

"Yes."

"We've got photography going in but he has a dog, and we can't find him. If you see anything let us know; the dog catcher is on his way."

"Yes sir, will do."

As he walked away, we gingerly got back inside the car but left the windows open. Not five minutes later, we heard the *pat-pat-pat* of paws on road and heavy panting—the sort that, even without looking, you just knew couldn't be a Chihuahua. To our left, a looming, heavy-set beast padded into the dark of a neighbouring garden like a lone wolf. (I thought it was a Rottweiler, though my colleague thought it was a German Shepherd.) It took an hour before the dog was caught and we were given the all-clear to go in.

Like many Massachusetts homes, the house had a wood frame. The entrance led into a lounge, which had been turned into an operations room and was busy with around five or six police officers milling about. An officer was taking names for the scene log at the door, but before we stepped forward, one of the Lieutenants abruptly said, "Stop!"

"What happened?" I asked cautiously.

"Careful of the dog," he said, nodding to the same giant pooch lying quietly on the floor.

That scene was the disappearance of Katherine Romano, which became the first Massachusetts murder case to be tried without a body.

Katherine was last seen on 27 September 1998 while working on the Big Dig, which was a tunnel project to build a freeway underneath the city of Boston. She lived in Quincy with Joseph Romano, though the couple were in the process of splitting up at the time. Her disappearance was reported, and an officer went to the house to talk to Joseph. He claimed that Katherine had up and gone, leaving their two-year-old son with him.

The officer asked to look around and found that things were out of place. That prompted the search warrant, and was why my colleague and I had been called in.

I left the scene 36 hours later, having managed a few hours of sleep somewhere in the middle of it all. The floorboards of the house were pulled up, revealing blood underneath them. We scraped the freshly painted walls to see if anything was underneath, scoured the large yard, basement, and any nook and cranny, and found a lot of blood but nothing more.

It was at some point towards the end of the scene work that a neighbour came forward with a Sawzall: a powerful electric reciprocating saw. He told officers that Joseph had borrowed it around the time Katherine had disappeared. It looked clean, but we seized it and took it back to the lab to be dismantled. Inside it were bone, muscle and tissue with DNA matching Katherine's.

In 2002, Joseph Romano was found guilty of second-degree murder. The jury accepted that Katherine was dead and had been dismembered, but decided there was not enough evidence to support a pre-meditated murder and believed it could have been a 'crime of passion'. It is thought that Joseph cut up the body with the saw and disposed of the pieces in the garbage.[7] Amidst all this, there was speculation that their two-year-old son, Bruno, had witnessed the whole thing.

---

[7]   See 'Quincy Man Charged in Wife's Killing', *Southcoast Today (via the Associated Press)* (1 January 1999) and 'Quincy Man Guilty in Death of Missing Wife', *Southcoast Today (via the Associated Press)* (1 June 2002). Available at https://www.southcoasttoday.com/article/19990101/news/301019979 and https://www.southcoasttoday.com/article/20020601/news/306019979.

The First Body

So far, we've been talking about issues in forensics and the nuts-and-bolts of the job, but there is also an emotional aspect to it.

Most of us see very few dead people in our lives, and the ones we do see tend to be either casualties in accidents or someone who died of natural causes, such as an elderly parent. In this job, depending on whether you go to crime scenes or not, you can end up encountering many dead bodies.

Being able to disassociate from the grim and violent situations we investigate is not something everyone can do. We all have our strengths and limitations, and although we can train ourselves to react in a certain way or to deal with things in the heat of the moment, that's very different from having to deal with them day in and day out.

Nor is it limited to just dealing with the literal *corpus delecti* (body of the crime). Even working in a lab setting, without actually seeing a body, can still cause significant trauma-related stress. For example, spending hours closely examining underwear from a young girl whom you know was brutally raped, tortured, and murdered isn't the same as reading about it in the news. The reality of the event has been brought right in front of you, and you are now part of that investigation, not a member of the public following a story.

As I've said, forensic work is not for everyone, but this is true of all professions. I couldn't be a plumber, given the sights and smells they often face. Some people are deathly afraid of electricity. I once met someone who desperately wanted to be a doctor but couldn't stand the sight of blood. (They naively thought they would get used to it over time but didn't, and ended up switching to a non-medical degree.) Similarly, I've encountered people who wanted to do forensics with all their heart, but couldn't get past the emotional impact of their first case.

When it comes to what we think we can withstand in a job like this, part of the conditioning process comes from growing up with exposure to things like TV shows or movies which show plenty of gore (through what I will concede are often excellent special effects), along with the thrill and drama of solving a crime. But it isn't like that on the job. You, the forensic scientist, rarely solve the crime. Most of your cases will be from people who have already been arrested as suspects, and your job is merely to catalogue, test and help verify what the police already believe is true. Take away the drama and all you're left with is the cold, stark and often sticky gore, smells and all.

It is easy to disassociate from the trauma of a real event which has been mediated through the newspapers or TV. We do it our whole lives when watching or reading the news. Some news stories or documentaries cover real and deeply shocking events, but because they didn't happen where we were, the emotional component of what we watch can be managed through what is in essence, denial.[1]

Post-traumatic stress is the mental processing which follows any traumatic event. Denial is a coping mechanism whereby we take stressful or traumatic events and believe they don't apply to us. Short-term denial is useful in that sense, as it calms our emotional response and allows us to absorb even horrifically shocking events until we are able to process them properly.

The same denial coping mechanism works well when dealing with a highly stressful situation, such as a bystander giving CPR to someone who has just been shot in front of them in the street, or, in the case of a crime scene investigator (CSI) attending the scene of a horrific death, calmly taking swabs from the still-warm body of the deceased. Denial allows us to function and get through what we need to until we can process the trauma later.

Post-traumatic stress disorder (PTSD) is what happens when short-term coping mechanisms fail to work. Denial may mitigate post-traumatic

---

[1]   Mayo Clinic Staff, 'Denial: When It Helps, When It Hurts', *Mayo Clinic Article* (9 April 2020).

stress until it is absorbed, but sometimes the shock and stress is never really dealt with and this compounds and persists, resulting in PTSD. Over time, this can have corresponding health and psychological effects.

The process can evolve slowly, as the horrors seen accumulate over decades and result in a breakdown later in life. Richard Shepherd, a well-known forensic pathologist in the UK, was diagnosed with PTSD after cutting up 23,000 bodies over 30 years.[2] This can be compounded by the existential questioning that accompanies a midlife crisis (as nicely summarised by Forbes),[3] which can arguably precipitate PTSD symptoms. The problem can be uniquely chronic.

Although post-traumatic stress can be managed with short-term measures, PTSD in forensics hasn't really been examined until very recently. In my own view, the bravado and stoicism that underpins our line of work means that, as professionals, we are expected to be tough, resilient and able to just get on with the job. After all, you can't turn up to a scene where three kids have been murdered and the mother is screaming in tears outside, only to burst out crying and fall to your knees. You have to save that for later—but when it comes to later, you're at another scene, and then another. By the time the weekend comes round, your denial mechanism has kicked in to try and help you have some semblance of a normal weekend, and that whole event coalesces into a slowly-forming mass of PTSD. The culture of stoicism lends itself to a culture of PTSD.

Much like emergency response services the world over (whether forensics, police, ambulance, fire, or military), the need to be calm in a crisis is part of the job, and many people in these roles are very good at it. Yet PTSD is more prevalent than we think. A 2004 study of ambulance

---

[2]   R. Lea, 'The Forensic Pathologist Who Got PTSD: 'Cutting up 23,000 Dead Bodies Is Not Normal', *The Guardian* (26 September 2018). Available at https://www.theguardian.com/science/2018/sep/26/forensic-pathologist-richard-shepherd-ptsd-cutting-up-23000-bodies-not-normal.

[3]   Forbes Coaching Council, '15 Signs You've Hit Your Mid-Life Crisis (and What to Do About It)', *Forbes* (31 August 2017). Available at https://www.forbes.com/sites/forbescoachescouncil/2017/08/31/15-signs-youve-hit-your-mid-life-crisis-and-what-to-do-about-it/?sh=7fde9797573c.

workers in the UK opined that around 22% suffered from PTSD, based on a sample of 617 responses.[4] A study by Rosansky which examined the coping tactics used by crime scene investigators in the US estimated that 10% showed sufficient distress to meet the threshold for PTSD.[5] Their coping strategies were basically a) just getting on with it; and b) learning to live with the stress.

The good news is that in recent times, 'well-being' has become a catch-phrase, and emergency response services are trying to explore, assess, and manage the mental health of emergency responders, especially after any major traumatic incident. For example, in 2018, the College of Policing (UK) produced a guide aimed at precisely this issue, titled *Responding to Trauma in Policing: A Practical Guide.*[6]

But in Massachusetts in 1997, when I worked on my first body, PTSD was something victims suffered from and well-being a drink with the team afterwards.

At the time, I was still doing my initial training as part of the lab's forensic chemist section, which included crime scene response. We didn't get called out to burglaries; if we were, it had to be something serious. It was inevitable that a day would come when I would have to shadow one of our experienced forensic chemists at a murder scene, and I had worried for some weeks about how I would feel and react when I saw my first body.

When that day came, I was lucky that my colleague Tina was on call. She had the calm authority of the teacher that everyone liked at

4   P. Bennett et al., 'Levels of Mental Health Problems Among UK Emergency Ambulance Workers', *Emergency Medicine Journal* 21 235–236 (2004). Available at https://doi.org/10.1136/emj.2003.005645.

5   J.A Rosansky et al., 'PTSD Symptoms Experienced and Coping Tactics Used by Crime Scene Investigators in the United States', *Journal of Forensic Science* 64(5) 1444–1450 (2019). Available at https://doi.org/10.1111/1556-4029.14044.

6   *Responding to Trauma in Policing: A Practical Guide*, UK College of Policing (2018). Available at https://paas-s3-broker-prod-lon-6453d964-1d1a-432a-9260-5e0ba7d2fc51.s3.eu-west-2.amazonaws.com/s3fs-public/2021-02/responding-to-trauma-in-policing.pdf.

school. It was a warm day with a haze in the air as we sped east towards Boston.

"You going to be okay?" asked Tina.

"Yes, I think so," I replied.

"Just watch and observe. If you have any thoughts or questions, let me know quietly. We don't need families knowing there's a trainee at their scene." (I hadn't even thought about how I might be perceived. I could only imagine how the news might report it: "State lab sends trainee to investigate father's murder!")

It was an hour's drive or so to New Bedford, where we pulled up outside a mom-and-pop style garage that I'd only ever seen in TV shows like *The Wonder Years*. It was late in the afternoon and the sun was casting a warm yellow glow around. It would have been cosy if not for the reason we were there.

The garage was an old, wooden-framed business with random car parts scattered around the place, not in a way that was messy, but which spoke to decades of being a sole mechanic at a family-run business.

We were met by a local detective, who said that the body was upstairs. He explained what they knew so far: the victim was an elderly man who had owned and run the store his whole life. He was very much part of the community, and would take in ex-offenders and people who had fallen by the wayside and give them work as an apprentice in his garage to try and keep them out of trouble. One of them, a known drug addict, was believed to have struck him over the head with a wrench and stolen the day's takings. The police were out looking for him already.

Tina looked around to see if anything was out of place while I followed her like a lost dog. After that was done, we walked up a creaky flight of stairs, made from old planks of wood and worn down from decades of use, into an upstairs workshop that smelled of engine oil. The room was long but quite narrow and the far end faced west, where sunlight was streaming through the dusty windows. On the right wall was a long workbench covered with tools like a large vice and drill press, and on the floor, close to the workbench, lay the victim on his side.

He was quite small, probably in his early 60s, and thin. He was dressed in a plaid shirt with overalls on top. The back of his head was matted with clotted blood and his glasses lay nearby his head, one of the lenses cracked. A large wrench lay conspicuously on the floor a short distance away. It struck me how sad it was.

We got to work. There was no one else around except myself, the detective, and Tina. At that point, she flipped control and made me direct the scene, asking me what I would do. I made some observations, and we took swabs and seized some items. A few hours later, we were on our way back to the crime lab at Sudbury, lit by the now-setting sun. As Tina later commented, it had been a simple scene and a good one for me to start with.

Over 20 years later, I can still feel the emotions I went through that day. Even writing about it brings thoughts of sadness, though I can't say whether this is PTSD or just the natural effects of any emotional shock that lingers in the heart and mind for eternity. It's just part of the emotions and tribulations of life.

I don't remember every case I've worked on. In fact, I remember relatively few of them in any detail. If someone showed me the file from a scene or incident it would probably come back to me, but not being able to independently recall any details is a good thing.

You might be wondering why some cases stick in the mind and others don't. To be honest, I don't really know. All of them involve people with family and loved ones, but some cases have a far deeper emotional impact. There are some cases that just have a profound feeling of tragedy and unfairness about them and go on to linger long afterwards, even if I couldn't tell this at the start.

Elizabeth Holland was murdered in her home on 13 October 1998 in Quincy, Massachusetts. I was called out to the scene alongside some excellent police officers, who diligently collected fingerprints while I took care of blood distribution and swabbing. Elizabeth was still lying upstairs curled up in her bed.

The story was that her estranged husband, Daniel Holland, broke into the house through a window, went upstairs, and shot Elizabeth eight times with a .22 rifle before beating her over the head with it. Their eight-year-old son, Patrick, slept through the whole thing, only to find his mother lying in her bed the next morning. I had seen plenty of bodies by then, some with horrific injuries, but for some reason this one just struck me with an enormous sense of tragedy.

Daniel Holland was found guilty of Elizabeth's murder in 2001, but appealed his sentence on the basis that his lawyers did not fully explore an insanity defence, based on a history of mental illness and drug abuse leading up to that night. However, the court rejected this, as Holland was evaluated by Bridgewater State Hospital and found not to be suffering from any major mental illness. He remains serving life without parole.[7]

There was a twist to this story: Patrick, the son, filed to have his father's parental rights terminated so that the couple who had been caring for him since his mother's death could legally adopt him. The case made international headlines, and in 2004, a judge granted the request. Daniel Holland waived his parental rights, and Patrick became another couple's son.[8]

---

[7]   L. Redmond, 'Ex-Quincy Man's Appeal of Wife's Brutal Murder Denied', *Patch* (19 April 2017). Available at https://patch.com/massachusetts/quincy/ex-quincy-mans-appeal-wifes-brutal-murder-denied.

[8]   J. Smith, 'Father Who Was Famously Divorced by His Son After the Boy Found His Dead Mother's Body Wants New Trial in Her Death Because He Says Lawyers Ignored His Mental Health Problems', *Daily Mail* (10 November 2016). Available at https://www.dailymail.co.uk/news/article-3922546/Killing-sparked-boy-divorce-dad-going-court.html.

The First 100 Bodies

I'd like to think I'm sufficiently capable of denial and dissociation in this line at work, but I, like so many of us, have limits. My wife can tell when something particularly bad has happened just by my face when I walk through the door. What's worse is that I can't talk to her about it, partly because she doesn't need to know the trauma I've had to deal with, but also because there are issues of both legal privacy and respect for the dead I must uphold.

Whilst working at the State lab, I dealt with a murder scene every few weeks, and so there was some natural downtime between the denial phase and working the post-traumatic stress out of my system. However, I soon realised that the only way to get ahead at the lab was if someone retired or left, and the job I'd started was aimed at recent graduates, not someone with several years' experience. I would have needed to jump up a rung or two to get to where I should be for my age, but the State lab had no provision for this. I started to look around for something higher up the ladder.

I had also realised that the American way of life was as tiring as it was compelling. American culture is very adept at deciding mid-week to have a barbeque and invite a bunch of people over, whereas in England you need to give everyone two weeks' notice. I loved the US' spontaneity and fun-loving way of life, but there was a downside: I got ten days of holiday a year, whereas in the UK I got at least 25. I soon learned that in the US, people worked all they could in order to pay the gardener, whereas the Brits just took a day off to prune the roses.

The thirst to travel and enjoy proper vacations had been needling me for some years. The eight-hour overtime granted each week to help ease the lab's backlog was financially welcome, but it meant I was working a six-day week on top of any call-outs.

I decided to look around, but I neither wanted to end up in another State lab nor to return to the UK, so I boldly made calls to the labs in the Bahamas, Bermuda, Barbados and Hawai'i. It was a long shot and as expected, there was nothing available. Then two weeks later, I caught an advert in the American Academy of Forensic Sciences employment bulletin: the Cayman Islands were looking for a forensic scientist.

In Cayman in 1998, interviews were done in person, which meant the Government of the Cayman Islands flew me to Grand Cayman and put me up for a night in a hotel.

Grand Cayman, which sits around 500 miles south of Miami, is the largest of three islands belonging to the Cayman Islands. My flight took me from Boston to Miami and then onto Cayman Airways, and an hour later we landed with a bump and some sharp braking (I later found out that the airport has a short runway). I stepped out of the plane into glorious sunshine.

The hotel I'd been given was 200m from the beach. I changed and went for a snorkel in what felt like bathwater. It was inspiring. Later, I spotted someone at the hotel bar who could only be another interview candidate and we got chatting. He was from the Drugs Task Force (DTF), and it turned out that all eight of the interviewees were being put up in the same hotel, split over two days.

At that time, Hurricane Mitch was battering the Caribbean (it killed 11,000 people, including 31 souls aboard the Fantome, which disappeared).[1] As a result, flights out of Cayman were cancelled, and the other group got stuck for an extra day. All of us bar one (we called him Mr. X) ended up going to the newly opened Fidel Murphy's Irish bar, which until recently had been a Cuban bar called Fidel Castro's.

Odd as it sounds, seven out of the eight competing interviewees ended up having a beer and dinner together, and we inevitably shared our

---

[1] J. Carrier, *The Ship and the Storm: Hurricane Mitch and the Loss of the Fantome* (International Marine/McGraw-Hill, 2000).

thoughts on how it went. One of the eight was Mike, whom I would meet again two months later when we restarted our careers by creating and then running a new forensic laboratory for the Cayman Islands.

There are things about island life that you need to get a grip on very quickly, lest you go crazy. We used to see this all the time. Expats—those who came to work in the Cayman Islands from another country—would have ideas about how to 'improve' things, were rude to the locals without realising it, and got mind-meltingly frustrated over how long it took to get things done.

Basically, the three-part guide to Caribbean survival—which likely applies to most islands around the world—goes as follows: be respectful, be flexible and find a hobby.

1. **Be respectful:** In my first week there, I called someone on the phone who answered with, "Good afternoon Sir, my name is Aisha, how are you today?" I immediately said, "Hi, I'm trying to reach so-and-so." Silence. I said, "…er, hello?," to which the woman gently repeated, a little more slowly, "I said: how are you today, Sir?"

   "Oh," I replied. "I'm fine, thank you. Um, how are you?"

   "So kind of you to ask Sir, I'm very well. Now, who do you need to speak to?"

   Got it. Always ask, "How are you today?"

2. **Be flexible:** If you want to earn people's respect, don't complain about how you'd get something done the same day in the US. You are on an island in the middle of the sea. Things take time. They take time to order. They take even longer to arrive. You will need to improvise. It's sunny. Chill out and have another Cuba Libre.

3. **Get a hobby:** Pick something you like to do and do it a lot. If not, you will fall into a vacuous alcoholic pit like those unhappy souls

who complain of having nothing to do on the island, and pour their money into rum and beer instead. I sailed, learned to scuba, played a little squash (yes, it was roasting hot), and wrote three full length murder-mystery fiction novels: *Compound Murder*, *Incendiary Man* and *Saving Lizzie* (all available on Amazon and other online retailers).

As for the lab, it was shoehorned into an office space which had been set up at the very back of the hospital, including the emergency generator, the hyperbaric chamber and the morgue. When we arrived, none of the analytical instruments had been used, so we had to write methods from scratch and do all the validations manually. We also needed more equipment.

It took several months of getting supplies and then performing validations to get the GC/MS and GC/FID online—we even had to pack our own GC column for the alcohol analysis—but the doors finally opened and the backlog of samples started to pour in.

Part of the service was offender urine drug screening. What I didn't appreciate was that the offenders would be walking into our building, and that we were the ones who had to collect the samples.

The building had two heavy doors which led to a hospital-wide corridor. People would knock or just walk in and we had no idea who they were or how dangerous they might be. In 1999, crack use was rampant on the island, and rehabilitating crack users can be as unpredictable as those who are still using it. Urine collections were done in a small bathroom just off the corridor that had a second door leading straight into the lab. At any given moment, the Cayman DTF might show up with bags of drugs for analysis while a drug offender was waiting to give a sample. Talk about putting a fox in the henhouse; it was inappropriate as it was insecure.

This wasn't the least of our worries. As a forensic scientist, I was expected to know how to take blood from people. This was news to me: until I met Mike in the Cayman Islands, I didn't know one that could.

Up till that point, it had been A&E doctors who took suspects' blood in drink-drive cases (when the suspect had refused or was unable to do a breath sample), but they no longer wanted to do it. Instead, the new forensic scientist would be taking over that role by being called into A&E, usually in the middle of the night, to take blood. Clearly Mike couldn't be on call every night, so I had to go in to—quite literally—watch someone else take blood and sign the forms.

It turned out that we also had to look after the morgue, with around a body a week. Sometimes they would appear in the fridges overnight, and we'd only find out about it when we opened each of the six chillers to check.

One day, the funeral home turned up to pick up a body. The person had died of natural causes, but the body had been laid in the morgue overnight without anyone filling in the book or letting us know.

That wasn't as embarrassing as the time the funeral home called, insisting that we had a body for them to collect, when we didn't actually have one. "I have the family sitting in my office arranging a funeral," the funeral director patiently explained to me over the phone. I told them I'd look into it, only to find out after a few phone calls to A&E that the man in question had arrived the night before in medical distress, been stabilised, discharged and sent back home. He was alive and well, but the 'marl road' (slang for gossip) had said he was dead, and the family hadn't even checked.[2] The marl road was like that–it could turn a living man into a dead one.

After two years in Cayman, I'd not only seen my 100th body but assisted in the autopsies of a portion of them. At the time, we had no full-time pathologist, and had to fly one in from Miami or Jamaica depending on who was available. The pathologist would normally stay overnight and come every one to two weeks, which sometimes meant a poor soul

---

[2] Marl is stone used to fill land and make roads. The 'marl road' is an unpaved road made from this stone,and a slang term for gossip.

would lie for over two weeks in the morgue before being released back to the coroner for burial.

After working on 100 bodies, seeing another was rarely an issue for me, but there were still those that triggered traumatic stress, such as cases of SIDS deaths (Sudden Infant Death Syndrome, or 'cot death') and another that I can't bring myself to write about involving a woman who died during labour.

The trauma of working in a morgue isn't as much about the emotional aspects of working with the deceased as it is about dealing with those who were left behind. In Cayman, we had to not only manage the body, but the loved ones who had to identify the body, sign papers, and take any personal effects. This might be a parent or partner, but with a lot of workers in Cayman being expats whose families were thousands of miles away, it was often a friend who had to step in.

Imagine a couple on holiday, getting off a cruise ship in the heart of George Town, Grand Cayman. The husband goes off to scuba dive while the wife goes shopping. They agree to meet later at 4:00PM by the jewellery store across from the cruise ship terminal.

4:00PM comes and goes and the wife stands patiently waiting. Eventually she sees two police officers walking towards her, and a lump comes to her throat as she is hit by a feeling of sudden dread: unable to fully comprehend what's going on, but knowing that something terrible has happened.

The officers ask her to go with them to identify a body. They take her to the hospital morgue, where she meets us, and we take her into a room where the deceased is lying on a stainless-steel autopsy table, covered with a sheet except for his face.

We had already gotten the pathologist's permission to take photographs and wipe the blood-stained froth from around his mouth and nose—caused by drowning—to make it look less horrific. We would normally have done the identification on a gurney away from the main autopsy room, but the trouble on that day was that the visiting pathologist happened to be on the island and would be leaving the next morning. If we didn't get the autopsy done that night, it would be another two weeks.

The woman nodded and confirmed it was her husband. I can still see the way she seemingly snapped and struggled to stand upright. We got her out to the entrance.

"What's going to happen?" she asked. I told her we were doing an autopsy. "Right now? Why? Can I not spend time with him?"

This wasn't a funeral home; it was a morgue, and this was a case of unnatural death. The body was the property of the coroner, and until the coroner was satisfied it could be released, access was restricted. The reason had nothing to do with the living, but respecting the rights of the dead: we might assume it was an accident, but the dead cannot tell us otherwise, which is why the coroner had to investigate. The police escorted the woman away to find a hotel and start the rest of her life, after everything had catastrophically changed an hour earlier.

Stories like this weren't uncommon. Cayman sees as many as ten water-related deaths a year, often involving tourists. Many are medically related, such as people who had heart attacks whilst snorkelling or diving, but some are both tragic and avoidable, such as the poor tourist who was accidentally left by a tour boat on the stingray sandbar in the middle of an ocean bay and drowned, or the teenager on a jet ski who lost control, ran over a boat, and killed his uncle.

There is also a high level of road traffic deaths. In 2018, Cayman had an average of six traffic accidents a day, and those were the ones that were reported. That year, eight of them were fatal.[3] You're about five

---

[3] J. Whittaker, 'One Year on Cayman's Roads: 2353 Accidents, 8 Deaths & 2,128 Speeding Tickets', *Cayman Compass* (2 May 2019). Available at https://www.caymancompass.com/2019/05/02/one-year-on-caymans-roads-2350-accidents-8-deaths-2120-speeding-tickets/.

times more likely to be killed on the roads of Cayman than you are in the UK.[4]

Add in deaths from alcohol, drugs, workplace accidents and gangs (which are responsible for most of the few murders per year in Cayman) and you have a fairly busy morgue, with almost every case involving grieving families, loved ones, or friends being escorted into the facility with the burden of identifying the deceased.

Raw, exposed emotion is different from the normal chatter of life. I think most of us can tell the difference between a scream for attention and a scream of terror. We can tell when people are upset versus when they are about to collapse because their world has fallen apart. I think we are conditioned to react when we hear or see such raw emotion as part of our evolved survival and nurturing instincts. Emotional detachment and short-term denial give us the ability to function calmly in moments of extraordinary stress.

Yet after most visits, when the morgue door closed and everyone had left, I'd take a moment to let the emotion shudder through me. You can't let it build up; you have to accept that it was awful, tragic and everyone has a right to be upset, including you. If not, you can get morose, bitter, cynical, quietly depressed, or possibly go crazy.

---

[4] M. Muckenfuss, 'Traffic Accidents Double over Two Years', *Cayman Compass* (25 February 2018) and *Reported Road Casualties in Great Britain: 2018 Report*, Department of Transport, UK (26 September 2019). Available at https://www.caymancompass.com/2018/02/25/traffic-accidents-double-over-two-years/ and https://assets.publishing.service.gov.uk/government/uploads/system/uploads/attachment_data/file/834585/reported-road-casualties-annual-report-2018.pdf.

Bunny Suit and/or Die

Bunny suits are the white disposable overalls you often see on crime scenes news. One of the better ones is Tyvek® by Dupont, but there are others ranging from economy to high-end. (This said, you don't really see them being worn on shows like *CSI: Miami* where, I suspect, editorial preference dictates that audiences would rather see characters' faces, makeup, coiffed hair, and nice clothing than a giant white penguin whose voice is muffled by a mask.)

Bunny suits are part of a set of personal protective equipment (PPE) and have various components, including a disposable lab coat, an elasticated coverall with separate trousers, and a one-piece that even includes covers for your shoes, attached to the bottom of the trouser legs.

If you've not worn a full suit, I'll give you an idea what it's like at the best of times.

The elastic hoops on the bottoms of the arms, which go over your fingers to keep the arms from riding up, will itch and give you friction burns on your hands.

The non-breathable suit will accumulate heat until it becomes an absolute distraction, which increases the risk of you missing something.

If you are unlucky, every type of mask will cause your glasses to steam up, no matter the time of year, causing you to be unable to see, which then becomes both a distraction and a safety hazard. You will end up fighting constantly with the mask and glasses, thus massively increasing the number of times you touch your face (and therefore risk defeating the whole point of wearing the mask).

The safety goggles will fight with your glasses (and even if you don't wear glasses, the goggles are invariably scratched and not fully transparent, so that you can't see 100% clearly).

The booties, or cover slips for your shoes, become like ice-skates if you step on anything wet, including blood.

Disposable gloves cause your hands to freeze in seconds, as I found out one night in Massachusetts when it hit around −12°C and I was trying to collect a sample of frozen blood off a sidewalk. But you can't collect swabs in ski gloves: in hotter weather, they accumulate sweat, and when you lift your hands, everything pours out of the cuffs.

Given all this, you might be wondering why we bother with bunny suits at all. It comes down to three things:

1. Protecting you from disease.

2. Protecting the scene from you.

3. Protecting evidence from other evidence.

Generally, crime scenes are static and inert. Lab examinations are even more so, with items already being days or weeks post-incident.

Autopsies are not. There's cutting into bone and tissue with a high-powered saw, manual incisions, manual sawing, open areas with body fluids, and sometimes—on top of all that—putrefaction. The autopsy team might be opening a cadaver that died from a gunshot, but we don't know if the person also had something like hepatitis B, tuberculosis or—as was a significant concern in the 1990s—a variant of Creutzfeldt-Jakob disease (CJD), the human equivalent of bovine spongiform encephalopathy (BSE), more commonly known as mad cow disease.

BSE is caused by a prion protein that lives in the spinal column and brain; it tends to survive for a very long time after death, and is hard to decontaminate. The mad cow epidemic started in 1986, when cows started showing a similar neural deterioration already known in sheep, called 'scrapie'. It was speculated the cows got it due to pieces of scrapie-infected sheep brain or spinal cord ending up in cattle feed.

Although cows seen to have this were required to be destroyed, some were still slaughtered for meat, and pieces of the brain and spinal cord ended up in food products for both animals and humans in the UK. As the 1990s rolled in, cats and zoo animals started to die after showing the same symptoms. In 1995, Stephen Churchill died of variant CJD.[1] It was serious because of how hard it is to get rid of.

There was also another threat that appeared around the time I was in the Cayman Islands: anthrax. Only a week after the 9/11 terrorist attacks in the US, anonymous letters containing anthrax spores—which can be deadly if inhaled—started to appear at the homes or offices of prominent figures in the US. The incidents went on for several weeks before they stopped, during which five people were killed and another 17 poisoned.[2]

The Cayman government was concerned that similar letters might have been posted to officials in the Cayman Islands, and so any unexpected letters to officials had to be tested for anthrax. Naturally, this enviable task was assigned to the forensic lab. We spent weeks testing envelopes and parcels—and thankfully didn't get a single positive anthrax case—but I was quietly alarmed at how many other spores and bacteria could be found on the outside of an envelope.

From a disease prevention perspective, the need to wear PPE is obvious, but at crime scenes and in controlled environments like a lab, wearing PPE is as much about preventing contamination as personal protection. It stops you leaving your DNA on an item or at a scene and prevents cross-contamination (i.e. transferring traces of evidence from one scene or item to another), though this only works if you change your PPE in between.

---

[1] See 'Timeline of Mad Cow Disease Outbreaks', Centre for Food Safety (undated). Available at https://www.centerforfoodsafety.org/issues/1040/mad-cow-disease/timeline-mad-cow-disease-outbreaks.

[2] 'Timeline: How the Anthrax Terror Unfolded', NPR (15 February 2011). Available at https://www.npr.org/2011/02/15/93170200/timeline-how-the-anthrax-terror-unfolded.

As DNA analysis becomes more and more sensitive, the chances of small, adventitious amounts of DNA cropping up keep increasing. Even in 2011, in a lab full of DNA experts, an innocent person was wrongly accused of rape when their DNA was picked up in a crime scene sample due to a disposable DNA tray being reused.[3]

For that reason, whether inside a lab or a major crime scene, forensic scientists or crime scene investigators in the UK are fully suited and booted. In the Caribbean, however, this poses another set of problems.

Despite what TV shows might have us think, most crimes do not take place in spacious, climate-controlled million-dollar homes with sweeping driveways and electric curtains. Most involve a slightly festering, cramped house with sticky floors and a pervasive, cloying smell that is a mixture of stale grease and cigarette smoke. In the Caribbean, any air-conditioning (if it is even on) is usually limited to the bedroom, and the whole flat can reach over 35°C (95°F) in the day even with the windows open.

Outside, the sun tends to beat down relentlessly on crime scenes, unless you are lucky enough to be in the shade. At night, the relative humidity soars, making you break a sweat just from blinking, whilst throngs of mosquitoes buzz loudly around your head. In the 1830s, Lord Sligo described Cayman's mosquitoes as "quite a national misfortune."[4] (When you account for the British understatement tempering that early 19th-century jab, you know it had to have been bad.) And if your scene was inside a boat or car, it could reach over 43°C (110°F) inside the cockpit, cabin, or whatever cramped space you needed to crawl into— heat that you could only sensibly bear for ten minutes at a time.

Now let's add PPE to that. The bunny suit traps heat and moisture, making any exposed areas of skin stream with large droplets of sweat

---

[3] Forensic Science Regulator, *Report into the Circumstances of a Complaint Received from the Greater Manchester Police on 7 March 2012 Regarding DNA Evidence Provided by LGC Forensics (FSR-R-618)* (17 September 2012). Available at https://assets.publishing.service.gov.uk/government/uploads/system/uploads/attachment_data/file/118941/dna-contam-report.pdf.

[4] M. Craton, *Founded upon the Seas* (Ian Randle Publishers, 2003).

that go flying as you move around. The double-layered nitrile gloves start to bulge with liquid as your hands try to release the heat through sweating. The moment you raise a hand above elbow height, sweat pours out in an unsightly stream onto whatever part of a crime scene you happen to be standing on. The outside of your PPE ultimately becomes contaminated by your own bodily fluids—one of the very things you are trying to prevent by wearing it in the first place.

Heat exhaustion—and if it progresses, heatstroke—become real and urgent considerations when wrapped in a plastic cocoon in the blazing sun. When your internal body temperature starts to rise, this can cause confusion, dizziness, and a pounding headache. If it progresses, it can also lead to seizures and unconsciousness.

For the CSI, wearing clean white or blue cotton clothing (along with a hair net, mask, booties, and gloves) allows the skin to breath and keep the CSI cooler, has no fibre risk (as 100% cotton white or blue cotton fibres are pretty ubiquitous) and reduces sweating, which reduces contamination risk of your DNA at the scene. Also, the clothing can be washed and reused.

It becomes a crime scene paradox. Wearing a bunny suit in extreme heat risks causing lapses in concentration, therefore leading to a poorer quality of work, a higher chance of contaminating a scene with your DNA, and serious health risks to the wearer. But if you don't wear one, it takes only a sharp lawyer or defence expert to point this out and make a show and dance of it in a trial, regardless of whether it made any scientific difference to the evidence.

In the end, legal expectations (status quo bias/expectation bias) forces the issue. The bunny suit goes on out of fear of legal repercussion, rather than as a pragmatic, risk-based solution that caters for both the welfare of the wearer as well as the scene.

Scene work wasn't the only thing the Carribean heat caused problems with; the other was the forensic lab. When we arrived in 1998, it turned out the lab had not been included in the planning process for the section of the new hospital that was still being finished. The air-conditioning system was designed on recirculating the air for efficiency and relied on a lower power compressor to drive it. However, you can't recirculate the air in a forensic lab, and the system was modified so that all the lab air was exhausted. In a single day, the compressor became too small to cool the room sufficiently.

In winter, the temperature hit 28°C (82°F) in the main lab, which wasn't helped by two gas chromatography ovens and an actual oven, but at least we could manage it. Then came summer, and by June it was 32°C (90°F) in there.

In the UK the Health and Safety Executive (HSE) would have forced us to close, but in 1999 in Cayman there was no such department. We simply did what we could.

The dress code at the Cayman Islands Hospital was business attire, but I could not comply with it. Some days I wore morgue scrubs because my own clothing would be soaked by 10:00AM and I needed to dry out. Some days I wore a T-shirt and jeans.

To add insult to all this, the air-conditioning kept tripping due to excessive use. With no cool air coming in at all, the temperature could hit 35°C (95°F). But the work needed to be done and we got on with the job until finally, around two years later, they upgraded the air-conditioning to a much larger unit.

Much as this sounds like hardship, at the end of the day, you could roll out the lab to the Seaview bar in five minutes, grab a dive tank and flop off the dock into beautiful coral-laden seas. After an hour roaming the wrecks and reefs, you climbed out, rinsed, and dried off in front of the sunset whilst sipping a cold beer. It wasn't so bad.

At least until September 2004, when everything changed.

SurvIVAN

June 2005, around nine months after the hurricane

I was sitting next to some guy in Miami airport, a place famous for its long meandering walks and food that can choke a donkey. I don't know how we got onto the topic, but I mentioned the Cayman Islands and he said, "Didn't you guys have a hurricane recently?"

"Yes," I replied.

He nodded thoughtfully, and with deep empathy, said, "I would love to be in a hurricane one day."

That got my attention.

"Er, really?" I answered, still wondering if my hearing wasn't playing tricks on me.

I could see he was looking sheepish, but he soldiered on. "Just to feel it, you know, the raw power of nature."

In a way, Mr. Stranger was right. The experience of feeling the raw power of nature, as he put it, is immeasurable. And it would never happen, as I pointed out to him.

"What you end up feeling," I said, "is the inside of hurricane shutters while the wind screams outside. You have no idea what is going on. You do get the sense that if you go out there is a reasonable chance of you dying. Then there is the aftermath. No fleets of trucks rolling down from the continental US with food, water and supplies. Bathing tastes of salt and bleach as you have to wash in sea water mixed with septic tank overflow with a dash of Clorox to sanitise it. You have no power for two months. And a plane taking off makes you cry." I paused for a moment to reflect. "I think that about sums it up."

He shifted his feet and sat on his hands, rocking back and forth. "Well, it would still be cool," he said.

I shrugged politely. *And you're an idiot*, I said to no-one.

Hurricane Ivan reached Grand Cayman on 11 September 2004. At the time, I had been living on a boat for around four years.

I have to admit: it's pretty cool to say you live on a boat. People often respond with comments like "Wow!" and "That's *amaaaazing*," and not without reason. There are times it *is* pretty cool to live on a boat. There is a certain simplicity that comes with that lifestyle: you can vacuum the place in ten minutes. Dishes cannot pile up in the kitchen. A toaster oven takes on new and exciting possibilities. And on a dark night, you can lie in your bed as the boat rocks in the wind and contemplate the universe in a way that, frankly, a queen bed in a condo just can't capture.

In reality, there are two types of people who live on boats. The first is the kind you are perhaps imagining, involving plush upholstery, gin and tonics, and hearty guffaws. It is where, at a click of the fingers, a servant dressed straight out of a J-Crew catalogue appears from behind a mahogany door bearing a silver platter of petit-fours. These are people who have boats they *can* live on, although they usually live in a mansion 3,000 miles away with rack storage for multiple family cars and blinds that close with an app.

And then you have the rest of us: the ones who make a lifestyle choice to live on a boat due to—let's face it—money. We can't afford to rent *and* own a decent boat, and life on board is no more glamorous than living in a caravan or mobile home. Once you pass the initial outlay, it's cheap, it's small; the toilet smells. Shower time is short as you can only carry so much water. If the air-conditioning breaks you will die in minutes. The kitchen is a twin-alcohol burner and a microwave. The fridge will stop working many, many times and the freezer box is so bad that ice-cream turns to slurry in 15 minutes (though this somehow did not deter me from buying it).

Even then, what you save in rent is not enough for boat life. Anything with 'marine' on it seems to start at US$50, even if it's just the label, and that's before paying a marine mechanic US$1,000 to pretend to fit it. Your savings go in the same place as the toilet tank (affectionately known as the 'holding tank').

For this reason, when the holding tank got blocked and filled up, I couldn't afford to pay someone US$1,000 to fix it. It was me who opened the inspection port, convinced that it was empty, only to find that it was not only full but under pressure. It was me who had to jigsaw an opening in the top to get a poo vacuum in (affectionately known as a 'pump out station'). It was me who then carried the holding tank outside and removed inch-thick brown slabs of limescale encrusted with—for want of a better word—*croutons*. Disgusting, you think? Oh yes, but then between gagging I would smile at the thought that I had saved a grand.

I bought the 10m (33ft) sailboat in 2000 at the recommendation of a good friend and long-time sailor, Bruce. After that, with some asking around, I found a dock at a house on a canal with owners who were happy to have a liveaboard in their back garden, and stayed at the bottom of their yard for the next six years. (I later found out that the owners had spent eight years aboard an official replica of Joseph Sloachom's 'Spray' and travelled the Caribbean.)

The house was a single-storey concrete home on a large lot and a canal that led to the bay. I liked the place, with its white picket fence and understated modesty. The front door was flanked by two terracotta lamps with bulbs that gave a sort of Halloween pumpkin effect year-round.

The owner was a tall, no-nonsense fellow with a deep, rounded radio voice that could control an army or lull children to sleep. When I asked if he had a dock to rent, the conversation went something like this:

"Hi, I got your address from someone who thought you might have a dock I can rent?"

"Well we do, but it's already rented." Awkward pause. "But I don't like him. If you give me a month's notice, it's yours."

Over the years, I became good friends with the owners and would house-sit to look after their cat while they were gone. This is how, to our great luck, my partner (later to be my wife) and I came to be house-sitting in September 2004.

The major downside of boat life in the Caribbean was the hurricane season. Every year, storm warnings would be raised and lowered. Squalls would slam through and heave the boat around. Tropical storms would pelt the deck with ball-bearing-sized drops of rain. And every year you wondered if this was it—if this was the one.

Our first few years passed without incident. Twice a hurricane came close, and we strung the boat in the middle of the canal with long lines only to find the storm had moved slightly and was no longer a threat. Hurricanes do that; a 100-mile deviation can change the outcome from devastation to a wet and windy but otherwise harmless day.

Major storms are tropical storms (winds >38mph) and hurricanes (winds >73mph), which are named by the National Hurricane Centre (NHC). They use a set of six names which are cycled in rotation unless one causes death or devastation, in which case it is withdrawn. Naming conventions run from A to W (excluding Q and U), thus covering 21 storms.[1] If a storm reaches sustained winds of over 74mph, it is also given a hurricane category on the Saffir-Simpson scale,[2] named after Herb Saffir and Bob Simpson, the two NHC employees who created it.

---

[1] See the 'About Names' page of the National Hurricane Center website. Available at www.nhc. noaa.gov/aboutnames.shtml.

[2] See the 'Saffir-Simpson Hurricane Scale' page on the National Hurricane Center website. Available at www.nhc.noaa.gov/aboutsshws.php.

The Saffir-Simpson scale has five categories, requiring sustained wind speeds as follows:

Cat 1   74–95mph

Cat 2   96–110mph

Cat 3   111–130mph

Cat 4   131–155mph

Cat 5   Over 156mph

Kinetic energy is the square of speed, so if you go from a low Cat 1 storm at 74mph to a low Cat 3 one at 111mph, the power of the storm more than doubles.

Hurricanes power up and power down as they progress, sometimes changing in category very quickly. Continual updates from NHC assessments, coupled with measurements from Hurricane Hunter planes that fly into storms, allow for scheduled updates on their intensity.

Both 2004 and 2005 were big years for hurricanes. There were 16 storms in 2004 alone, with four (Ivan, Jeanne, Karl and Lisa) active at the same time at one point.[3] The satellite image looked like the space station scene from *The Day After Tomorrow*.

A week before Hurricane Ivan struck the Cayman Islands, I was in Tampa, Florida visiting a friend. I couldn't fly home on Sunday as Tampa airport was closed, due to the remains of a former hurricane (now the powerful tropical storm Frances) passing overhead.

---

[3] See the entry for 2004 at the 'Tropical Cyclones' monitoring page, maintained by the US National Oceanic and Atmospheric Administration. Available at https://www.ncdc.noaa.gov/sotc/tropical-cyclones/.

Monday morning was much the same: wet, wild and darkly foreboding. Tampa airport was still closed, but oddly, it was possible to rent a car. The local weather Doppler radar (an instrument which measures how fast rain is moving) showed that despite the mayhem outside, if I could make it just two hours south, I would be cruising among blues skies and along dry roads.

Cayman Airways switched me to a flight out of Miami, and an hour later I was rolling out of Tampa International Airport onto Interstate 75. It was not an easy drive, but then I'm from the UK, where driving in horizontal pelting rain while gusts of wind shunt the car around is called a bank holiday. You just put on lights and wipers, peer into the daytime darkness and drive at 30mph. I was virtually the only car on the road anyway.

A long two hours later I emerged from a wall of rain into searing sunshine. I smiled, found a ubiquitous classic rock station, put my foot down to Miami airport, and landed in Grand Cayman on the evening of Monday 6 September 2004, a day late and a few dollars lighter. My partner, Monica, handed me a message from a lawyer asking me to call him; we were ready to close on a condo.

Despite the idyll of boat life, we had decided to finally get a place to live, although the condo wasn't perfect by any stretch of the imagination. The sofas were sticky, the windows were crusted white with corrosion (common in the Caribbean as a result of the salt-laden air), and the kitchen bordered on chemical warfare. It could have doubled for most of the crime scenes I'd been to. It needed a complete refit, but I was up for a project.

On Tuesday, I popped into the lawyer's office, which was in a nice building downtown with a wonderful view of the giant and ever-growing landfill. I signed around nine pieces of paper which had little self-sticky arrows with the words "SIGN" printed on them. We shook hands and I asked, "Is that it?"

The lawyer nodded. "We just need to get them to the registry, which will happen today. Oh, and here's the key."

Monica and I went by the place, held hands, and smiled. We had dreamed of living by the ocean. The upstairs main bedroom opened onto the rolling seas; with the windows open, you could hear the sound of the waves and smell the salty sea-life. We changed the locks (because you never know if someone might want to steal a cockroach-infested kitchen cabinet), and as we left, we noticed a small, metal wind chime hanging on the covered porch next to the front door. It jingled melodically as if saying "hi."

The next morning, I was on a flight to Ohio.

For every year since the year 2000, I had submitted costing for adding a DNA lab to our existing forensic suite at the Cayman Islands hospital. Nothing came back until 2004, when it turned out that someone else had had the great idea to build a DNA lab for the island (really, where were all my proposals going?). Suddenly, things were a go, and we were trundling down the double-helix path.

In the world of forensic science, once an organisation so much as mentions DNA, the rest of the hard-working, non-DNA scientists know they will soon be facing some stark realities at work, namely:

1. DNA will take up at least three times more space than it was thought was needed.

2. Non-DNA departments will be shrunk or closed.

3. Non-DNA scientists will hope to keep their jobs, or worse, be made to learn statistics *and* genetics in order to become DNA scientists and keep their jobs.

In Cayman, we already knew we had no space and other sections would have to compromise. Staffing wasn't much of an issue as we only had funding to hire one person. The question was whether we could create an accredited forensic DNA lab in the space we had with only one employee. Could we create what was possibly the smallest accredited forensic DNA lab in the world? I had no idea, but part of the answer lay in Ohio.

Not far from Cleveland was an accredited, single-employee DNA lab that was happy to show us how they made things work. With a few hundred thousand dollars at stake, it was worth checking it out, and so a trip was arranged for me, the Police Commissioner, the director of the Cayman Islands Hospital, and the hospital's head of facilities.

We flew out on 8 September 2004 into a dark and foreboding Ohio sky. "I recognise that cloud," I thought, and turned on the weather channel. Sure enough, the remnants of Hurricane Frances were sitting over my head once more.

Over breakfast the next morning, no-one was talking about the lab we were off to see. There was only one topic: Hurricane Ivan, churning its way across the Caribbean Sea on a collision course with Grand Cayman. We could picture the scene back home and feel the tension mounting. It was not a good time to have the hospital director and Police Commissioner off the island.

Denial is a big factor in many crisis situations. So many storms come close and veer away; surely this would do the same. But something was different with Hurricane Ivan. Its course was true and unbending; it seemed to have conviction and purpose. We kept trying to get earlier flights, but there was nothing out of Ohio until Friday morning.

And so it happened that on Friday 10 September 2004, a day before Hurricane Ivan struck, I was sitting in my Ohio hotel room with some continental chocolates in one hand and a gourmet filter coffee in the other, wondering what mayhem was going on back home. I felt pangs of guilt, thinking that I should be on the ground getting ready for battle (though it didn't stop me eating the chocolates or drinking the coffee). At that moment, part of me felt there wasn't much I could do anyway, not to mention that it might be the last coffee and chocolates I would be eating for a while. It turned out that that was only half-true.

We landed in Miami the same Friday morning. Calls were made and strings were pulled; Grand Cayman was in the throes of a mass evacuation of all non-essential persons (mainly families and tourists). All regular flight schedules were cancelled, and Cayman Airways was operating shuttles back and forth. Getting seats on a plane to Cayman wasn't tricky; everyone was heading *out* of Cayman except us. The issue was whether there would be one more flight going back there.

We waited and waited, then it was announced and we ended up on the last flight heading to the island for evacuation, with only the crew and us few souls on board.

There was something refreshingly naïve about having no idea what was going to happen. Back at the lab, we followed the hurricane preparations, including checking for items on floors and moving them up in case of flooding. The urine analyser, Infrared spectrometer and both Gas Chromatographs were powered down and the security checked. Per the hurricane response plan, a 12m refrigerated container was delivered to the end of the building in case of mass fatality requiring body storage. There was a busy nervousness about the place.

On Saturday, we made our preparations at home. The boat was strung with ropes in the middle of the canal, the yard was cleared of furniture and things that could blow away, and the concertina hurricane shutters were closed, leaving the place in twilight. By 4:00PM, the sea swell ahead of the hurricane had pushed the water in the canal within a few inches off the top of the dock, and ominous rolling waves were starting to crash on the south shore.

In the evening, we were joined by a couple of friends who had been evacuated from their beachfront home. We ate a decent dinner and, by 9:00PM, settled in to watch a *Pink Panther* box set I had picked up as an anxiety purchase in Miami airport. The wind outside was rising to a moan and the shutters were rattling, but we had wine and a movie. Then the power went out and stayed that way for two months.

Oddly, my first thought was that it was a shame we didn't get to finish the movie. My second was to figure out where we had left a flashlight so I could use it to find the candles. And then I realised the next problem: the house ran off cistern water pumped from under the house, so no power meant no water pump, and no running water. There was one flush left in each of the toilets.

We sat in the dark and chatted while things got louder outside. At that stage, it was still more or less like a really inclement day in the UK, but with less power. Eventually, we decided we should try and get some sleep, made last checks around the house, and put our heads down at around 1:00AM.

I woke around 3:00AM. Things didn't seem so bad; there was no real change from two hours earlier, but I decided to do a perimeter check. Armed with a flashlight, I padded down the corridor, where the *pad-pad* of feet on tile turned into a *plosh-plosh* as I reached the dining room. Water was running across the floor, but it was coming from the higher part of the house in the kitchen, down into the lounge, and out the back door, where the canal was. In other words, the water wasn't coming from the canal.

I tried to picture the scene outside, but it made no sense. Why would water come from the road in such a quantity that it was pouring through the house *into* the canal?

I later found out that just over a mile away to the south, the rolling waves we had seen at 4:00PM were now goliath monsters reaching up to 6m (20ft) high, crashing over the shoreline. As they had nowhere to retreat, the water was cascading across the low-lying areas to the north until it drained back at the other side of the island, where we were. From the air, the island would have looked like it was cleaved in two.

Meanwhile, with the flooding, a serious and foreboding liquid started rising in the tubs and toilets. This is what sanitation teams call 'black water': the liquid that the septic system produces as sewage passes from the confines of a tank into the big world. It looked thick and ugly, like black soup.

We hoped it wouldn't go over the bathtub, and to be honest, had it been a proper UK-style one, we would have been fine. American bathtubs, by contrast, are a breach of trade description: they are so small you cannot bathe in one. In fact, they serve no purpose unless you want to wash a baby or a dog. Thanks to the tub's top lip being so low, the black water was pouring over it like a scene from a horror movie.

What I didn't know was much the same was happening in the forensic lab. The same giant, crushing waves on the south shore had forced deep flood waters to surge down a huge section of lowland that ran from sea all the way to the back of the hospital. The seawater, mixed with a multitude of overflowing septic tanks, debris and swamp mud, was coursing through the rear of the hospital and leaving the forensic lab two feet deep in muddy, sewage-infected salt water.

Back at the house, it was clear that beyond the seemingly impenetrable walls and shutters, all hell was breaking loose outside. The wind whistled and groaned like a banshee and the shutters rattled furiously, but all that banging and crashing was just the beginning. The wind beat against the concrete wall in a strange rhythm, while the wall itself periodically shuddered in response to a new high note in the screaming. I couldn't imagine that things would get worse, but somehow, they did.

You know that scene in *Jurassic Park* when the T-Rex is getting close, causing the coffee cup to vibrate and little ripples to form in the liquid? That was the bedroom wall, except the whole thing felt like it was rippling. Although the shutters were closed and the windows were cranked shut, I could feel a fine mist of water on my face as I got closer. The sheer pressure of the wind was driving the rain through. And sure enough, the entire wall was vibrating. By this time, the wind was screaming like the amplified drill of a maniacal dentist, followed by a heavy pounding on the wall like God trying to knock. At this point, we lost our nerve and sloshed through the flooded rooms into the kitchen, where we sat for several hours until things calmed a little.

The hurricane-force winds persisted for much of the daytime on Sunday and into sunset, so it was Monday before we ventured out of the house. Everything had changed in the last 48 hours. The streets looked post-apocalyptic. Power lines snaked everywhere like dead tentacles, trees and bushes were strewn across the roads, and everything was blanketed with debris from damaged houses. Cars were filled with seawater up to steering-wheel height; the tin garden shed was torn up like paper; roof shingles were impaled horizontally into wooden telephone poles. We'd thought we had it bad, but we still had something of a roof.

Someone asked if I had lost the boat. "No," I said. "I know exactly where it is."

Our floating home was now impaled onto the remains of a dock post. The stake had been driven right through the bottom of the bow, leaving the front of the boat sticking up out of the canal like a harpooned whale and the whole aft section, the area towards the stern, underwater.

The first thing we did was to check on the elderly couple next door. There were no signs of life out front, so we nervously walked around the back, only to find them with their kitchen-sized barbecue running. With a ready smile, the lady who lived there asked if we'd like a coffee. It would have been almost normal if not for how a third of their roof was missing. The worst thing, she told me years later, was that when the roof blew off along with the ceiling, they could see dozens of rats running around the rafters, trying to escape the flood waters.

We did what we could that first day, and, after sunset, padded around in the dark with candles. We fetched buckets of 'water' from the breached cistern tanks under the house to wash in, but it was now mixed with seawater. There were even little fish swimming around. We added bleach to each bucket and used it to wash. For days, our skin tasted like chlorine and salt.

That night there was silence. No night birds, no roosters, no frogs, no cars, no dogs barking, no overhead fan. The air was clammy and still and felt like a weight on the chest. I moved around, probably trying to make the air move, but it didn't help.

Then came the smell, putrid and choking. I lay there in disbelief. It was obvious what was causing it: every house in the area used a septic system. I bet most of them had overflowed like ours, and their contents were now oozing over the grounds, houses and bushes.

Exhaustion eventually took its toll. When I woke, it was to the first glimmers of light outside. I felt just as tired and burned out as the night before, but shoehorned myself out of bed in the dim light and made coffee using our little barbeque (the house had no gas or propane).

I had to get to work somehow. After a quick breakfast, I jumped in the house owner's Toyota pickup truck, which started with a groan, and drove off towards the Prospect hurricane shelter. The emergency radio broadcast had been asking for spare pillows and blankets. I grabbed some and threw in two towels as well.

The back road to the shelter didn't seem too bad. For the most part, it was clear of debris and power lines. I could see people walking around, some looking busy, and others like they were in a scene from a zombie movie. There was a sort of emptiness about the place. No cars on the road, no smiles or curious glances when I drove by, just a lot of stern faces and sunken eyes.

The houses had fared much the same; some were missing roof parts, while others looked intact. The drone of a generator could be heard here and there. I turned onto the new road up to the shelter, a primary school building on which construction had just finished. I wondered if it had even seen any classes. As I pulled up, there was a reassuring air of calm and order.

I was met by a man at the front who took the blankets and pillows. "How are things?" I asked.

"Better than you might think," he said. "We got air-conditioning and no flooding, plus plenty of water."

His comment made me smile. I turned to leave, and a middle-aged British couple asked where I was going.

"Heading to the hospital," I replied. "Why?" They asked if I could drop them at the end of the road, up by Mariners Cove.

It made no difference to me. "Sure," I said, and they hopped in. The truck started (although, to be honest, it sounded less happy this time) and we drove up the road.

The couple were from Sheffield and had lived in Mariners Cove, a sprawling condo complex next to the ocean with a fantastic dock and natural harbour right at its feet, for many years.

They looked tired. "Have you been up there?" the man asked me.

"Not yet," I said. There was something heavy in his tone, and I remembered the radio had mentioned the road had been completely blocked. I shot him a questioning look.

"The whole of Mariners Cove has gone," he said, matter-of-factly. It turned out that unlike almost all the other concrete condos on the island, this one was all timber-framed. It had been flattened to slabs.

"All we have is what we arrived at the shelter with. Passport, wallets, a few clothes," he continued. Sadness hung in the air as we reached the main road. We drove on, past some houses with scratches and war wounds but looked otherwise all right, and reached the T-junction with the East End Road.

Ahead, over the main road, there should have been a large pink-coloured condo complex. What I saw was debris-covered tarmac with nothing beyond it except the corner section from a single condo, which gaped open to reveal a closet with a few pieces of clothing still hanging on the rail. It was such an odd sight. (I later met the person who owned the clothing, and yes, she did get it back. According to her, it was even dry.)

To my right, giant bulldozers had unceremoniously carved a road through what had been a mountain of rubble, roof and walls. Much of it had been forced into the bushes as a giant slope of trash, and 30 or so people were picking through the debris.

"That's what we're going to do," he said with a frown.

"Really?" I asked.

It was a stupid question, but he replied anyway. "I don't think we will find our stuff, but if we could just find some clothes to wash, that would get us through," he said.

My heart sank. I wished them luck and turned the pickup around.

I wound my way through the back roads to the main road to town, which had been cleared barring a few high voltage cables. It felt odd driving over them, as if I had crossed a strict boundary between safety and death by vaporisation. Other than that, driving was better than I hoped and I soon arrived at the hospital's main entrance.

The hospital looked, for the most part, normal. There were people milling around and a sense that things were being done. The hospital had been occupied and 'open' (insofar as that applies in a hurricane) the whole time, so I suspect people had been busy doing more of the same for the last two days. I said a few hellos and went upstairs to management to see what was what. After being redirected a few times, I reached someone who wrote my name down in a book to show I had turned up for work.

As I headed back out, I saw a familiar face. The week before, we had had an autopsy for a road traffic case, and Dr. B had flown in from

Jamaica to do it. Dr. B was a youthful, smooth-skinned Jamaican who always had a smile and a calm air about him. That day, he looked shattered.

"Aren't you supposed to be in Jamaica?" I asked.

He shrugged. "By the time I was finished here, Jam was closed by the hurricane so I couldn't get home."

I hadn't realised that the hurricane had hit Jamaica before us. I wondered if he'd heard from his family, but none of us had a working phone. It struck me that they must have been frantic with worry about each other, but I left it at that. His weary expression said it all.

"They looking after you?" I said, changing the subject.

"Not bad, not bad," he replied with a shrug. "Best they can do." I said my goodbyes and made my way towards my lab at the rear of the hospital.

I bumped into one of the A&E staff on the way. It was a small hospital, and many of us knew each other by sight if not by name. She looked tired but still managed a smile. After a quick chat about what had happened, she nodded her head in the direction of my lab. "Have you been down there yet?" she asked.

"Just heading," I answered.

She shook her head. "I heard the whole place was flooded. We lost power for hours as they had to shut the generator down as it was going to flood. Even physio got flooded at the back." That wasn't a good sign; their building was a few feet higher than ours. I thanked her and carried on.

The forensic lab was in a building connected to the main hospital by a sheltered outside corridor. The whole thing looked fine: wet, but otherwise fine. With a little more optimism, I walked down the concrete ramp to the entrance of the lab.

As I got to the end of the ramp, I could see the refrigerated container at the other end of the building, about 30 metres away from where it originally was. The thing looked like someone had being playing dice with it. I went around our building to the rear parking lot, which was filled with cars pointing in random directions and a brown layer of mud which ran several feet up the building wall. I later heard from a nurse who had worked through the hurricane that a tidal wave had come through the back of the hospital so fast, it had picked up the container and rammed it down the entire line of cars which had been carefully parked behind our lab.

With a heavy sigh, I clambered across a bunch of debris and opened the back door into the forensic building. Inside, the emergency lights were on, but it was still dim. Without the air-conditioning, the air inside was hot and heavy, with moisture so thick it felt like rain. I could see the band of mud two feet up the walls. I took a right into the morgue, which was also barely lit, and it was the same story: thick black mud in a line so neat as though someone had painted it on purpose. I checked the tap and there was no water.

I went out to the corridor and unlocked the office. It was pitch black inside. I gingerly rescued the pet Siamese fighting fish, put his bowl into the corridor, and opened the lab. It was the same thing: mud, mud, and mud, and the same pervasive sulphur smell that was everywhere but another ten degrees hotter. Sweat was already dripping off my head. The reagent fridge was upturned and had spewed thousands of dollars of materials over the floor. The US$60,000 urine analyser stood just next to the door with the same brown line of mud across its middle.

I decided to check the small exhibit room, which had a tall fridge and freezer in it. It was the same thing but hotter and smellier. The flood had toppled both the fridge and freezer and emptied hundreds of vials of blood and urine across the tiles. Thankfully nothing had broken, but some of the urine vials had clearly leaked. It was disgusting to look at, not to mention the smell of stale urine which now mingled with the overall sulphur and rank. It would all have to be thrown away, along with boxes of archived material on the shelves which were now a sodden mess.

I turned back and headed out. As I was leaving the lab, I grabbed one of the lower lab drawers out of curiosity and tugged it. It was stuck, but finally made a small splash and moved an inch. I couldn't fault the workmanship. Who'd have thought the drawers would still be full of water?

And that was all I could take. The enormity of the situation fell on me like a tombstone. It wouldn't have been too bad with many hands on deck, but there were none to be had. People at the hospital were dealing with repairs, lack of power and water, patient injuries, maternity, pharmacy, and all the usual critical hospital functions. I sensed it was just going to be me. I later turned out to be mistaken, but in the moment, despair took me.

I went back to the pick-up truck, which, as if sensing the mood, almost didn't start. The engine rolled over like a tranquilised elephant, but by luck it fired and I drove home. It didn't run again until we got a new starter motor months later.

At home, my wife Monica was still outside. Somehow, she had managed to transform the chaos of fallen trees, brush, and branches in the yard into neat piles ready to be disposed of. I cocked my head in wonder, and then saw one of the Honduran fishermen in the corner of the yard swinging a machete like he was born with it attached to his arm. With each chop he split and cleaved, working through the remaining debris like a robot. It was something to see.

I thanked him and asked if there was anything I could get him. He looked down at his tanned, bare feet and said, in Spanish, that he'd lost his shoes. I took off a sandal and put my foot next to his: same size.

"No problema," I said with a smile. I got up, fetched a pair of leather deck shoes and handed them over along with a warm beer. His grin said it all. This was the reality of post-hurricane survival.

As truly disgusting as the night-time smell and heat were, we were so exhausted that the mornings came quickly, and I would find myself padding around the house not long before the sun came up. It occurred to me that this was how civilisations lived before the discovery of fire. You had to make use of all the light available.

After a few days, we went to look at our newly bought condo. The complex was mostly still standing, but all the oceanfront ones were hollowed out. The garden and pool areas were mounds of twisted fridges, sinks, cabinets, sofas, and even some cars. The sea had smashed straight through them, leaving the upstairs still standing as if each had been built on stilts.

In our unit, the solid wood front door had been torn in half like it was paper. Half the stairs were missing. The kitchen, lounge furniture, cabinets, and patio door had been replaced by a reasonably large piece of brain coral. Oddly, next to the remaining half of the front door, the little wind chime was still tinkling in the breeze, so we took it back to the house as a symbol of hope and endurance.

Thankfully we had never moved in, but a couple who lived there arrived at the same time we did, took one look, and burst into tears. They'd lost everything.

Each day brought a whole set of things to do: cleaning, fixing, repairing vehicles, getting water or food, helping other people, trying to stay focused. At work, we managed to get running water after a few days, around the same time the airport reopened for daylight traffic only. The simple growl of a turbo-prop Cayman flight heading over the bay brought a tear to my eye; the island was finally being re-connected to the world. Soon after, various countries sent flights to repatriate their citizens.

Every day there was a slight change or improvement. The supermarkets started to open; petrol became available; the car parts place reopened; a restaurant started serving food (with two menu options: take it or leave it) and workers were flown in to start piecing the island back together.

After two weeks, the forensic lab got its lights back on, but we couldn't use any sockets safely. It took six weeks to get a crane big enough to pull my boat out of the canal and leave it in the backyard to be repaired. After two months, we got our power back on in the house.

It's hard to describe how life goes in the aftermath of a national disaster, but as I write this, the COVID-19 pandemic has engulfed the world, and the challenges like getting food and supplies, curfew, isolation, and unemployment, are similar. Most of you reading this will now have had a taste of what this is like. So picture that, and then add a lack of power, internet and running water and that's much how it was for the first few weeks. Life was lived day by day.

I was lucky I worked at the hospital. It had running water and a shower. The police weren't so lucky, as their headquarters had to be closed and a temporary HQ set up in another building.

Crime became a huge problem, with a mix of emotion and desperation leading to plain old opportunistic looting. Armed police kept supermarket lines in check. The police also still needed forensic support, but we were in no condition to provide any lab service. The most I could do was help take swabs and samples from those arrested for processing later. Somehow or other, forensic support needed to go on, despite a lab that had no live power sockets and two feet of mud up the walls.

In the end, we did what we could. All the equipment was moved, and eventually a team (mostly from Mexico) came and replaced the lower sections of the damaged drywall. It did look odd for a few weeks: if you stood up you felt like you were in a room, but once you crouched you could see to the other end of the building.

Drugs were still being seized. To try and mitigate the mountain of cannabis and crack that was certainly going to pile up, we reached out to our Caribbean neighbours for help, and the Bahamas answered our calls. They said they couldn't spare people, but we were welcome to use their lab, and so once a month, armed with around two large rucksacks full of illicit substances, the exhibits officer and I would board the Tuesday BA252 flight to Nassau and get picked up at Lyndon Pindling International Airport by the drugs unit. By Friday, we would be heading home.

In between, we would manage to weigh and analyse a hundred or more drug items. If I was lucky, I got a few hours off to stretch my legs and see the town, but normally it was all just a mad dash which ended with grabbing the last printouts on the Friday morning and legging it back to the airport.

Even as we kept some semblance of forensic support going on in Cayman, the lab had to be rebuilt, a new urine analyser purchased, all of the equipment retested, and then all the methods re-validated. The only positive in this whole exhausting and soul-shattering experience was that with the lab benches, walls and electrics all needing to be redone, we made the physical layout changes we needed for the DNA lab without any real interruption to services. It was thus out of the ashes of Hurricane Ivan that the DNA lab was born and eventually became accredited several years later, after I had left.

As for how the Cayman Islands fared in terms of fatalities, the official death toll from Hurricane Ivan was two, but the actual number was three. (I never found out why this was, but I suspect one of the deaths had been categorised as 'natural'–i.e. not caused by the hurricane–whereas the other two were found weeks afterwards.)

What wasn't counted were the indirect deaths. It was obvious that some people wouldn't have died if not for the hurricane, such as the two poor souls who died from carbon monoxide poisoning from using a generator inside their condo (it was suspected they were worried it might be stolen if left outside). Others were less directly linked, such as the increase in suicides, and those who died due to infection and disease that probably wouldn't have happened had hygiene levels across across the island not been so badly compromised.

The connectivity of things is often hard to assess. What might cause someone to commit suicide or die from an amniotic embolism might be so far removed from its root beginnings that we simply can't join the dots that far. By way of example, nine months after Hurricane Ivan, while on my first trip back to the UK to see my parents, a section of the eyelashes on one of my eyes fell out. There was a neat rectangular gap about half a centimetre wide on the top lash line. A few weeks later they all grew back, but this time they were white. The effect extended upwards into my hairline. There was only one real reason why it had happened: this was my little memento of a hugely stressful event, perhaps even a physical manifestation of PTSD.

I left Cayman in 2006 to return to the UK and went back to being (mostly) on the dark side. After so many years of working for the prosecution, it was a huge transition, starting with a problem that prosecution experts rarely encounter: disclosure, i.e. getting to see the actual evidence.

As for hurricanes, the UK rarely sees anything like that, and even less so in the northeast of England, but for years after Hurricane Ivan, a stormy, windy day made me slightly anxious.

Disclosure and the Expert

In England and Wales, the civil rules of disclosure are well-documented and stringently followed. They are just as clear on criminal matters: specifically, the Crown must serve any material it feels might benefit the defence or undermine their case, and list all material that has been looked at (even if not used at the time it was listed) as 'unused material'.[1] Following these steps, however, is a different matter.

The investigating bodies—mainly the police, but including others like the Health & Safety Executive—will look under various stones and turn up an array of evidence. Most of this will be extraneous material which will not further the investigation, but there can be some that might help the defence or undermine the prosecution without the investigating officers knowing it at the time. It's for this reason that disclosure is so important. As the chair of the Criminal Cases Review Commission commented in 2018:

> "All those involved in criminal justice know we have a major problem. I drew particular attention to non-disclosure in my 2015/16 Annual Report and I wrote to the Law Officers, Director of Public Prosecutions and the National Police Chiefs' Council urging action. It is why I referred to non-disclosure at our 20th Anniversary Conference as 'the biggest single current problem' affecting the right to a fair trial."[2]

The truth of cases is sometimes wrapped up in unused material. Unless anyone else is given a chance to look at it, the truth might simply be held out as speculation or written off as the defendant's lies. In a way, that is the saddest part: defendants can be telling the truth *and* have

---

[1] See the 'Disclosure' page of the Criminal Prosecution Service website. Available at https://www.cps.gov.uk/about-cps/disclosure.

[2] R. Foster, 'Comment Piece by CCRC Chair Richard Foster', *Criminal Cases Review Commission* (18 January 2018).

evidence to support it, but prosecution might not have taken it on board, investigated it or served it.

For the most part, I don't believe this is done on purpose. I know that in some cases, confirmation bias or role bias may lead to hiding facts which do not fit the Crown's theory. However, the greater issue is a fall in the number of people working in criminal prosecutions at the same time as an explosion in digital evidence. There are literally not enough heads between the police and Crown Prosecution Service (CPS) to investigate all these channels, let alone get full disclosure done. Even if the police complete their disclosure in time, there's a good chance it will end up stuck with the CPS.

On top of this, the arrival of the General Data Protection Regulation (GDPR) has contributed to a climate of paranoia.[3] Officers are so fearful of committing a breach of data privacy that they will refuse to disclose data or material to the defence, even when their own expert has used it to write a report for the Crown. This occurs despite an exception in the GDPR legislation, which specifically says that it doesn't apply if "processing is necessary for the establishment, exercise or defence of legal claims or whenever courts are acting in their judicial capacity."[4]

Disclosure has made headline news in recent years. In 2018, the Director of Public Prosecutions apologised for 47 rape/sexual offence cases that were halted because the Crown had not properly disclosed the evidence, noting that disclosure was a "long-standing systemic issue."[5] That same year, Parliament launched an inquiry into the matter.[6]

---

[3]   General Data Protection Regulation 2016/679 (effective May 2018).

[4]   GDPR Article 9(2)(f).

[5]   C. Davis and V. Dodd, 'CPS Chief Apologies over Disclosure Failings in Rape Cases', *The Guardian* (5 June 2018). Available at https://www.theguardian.com/law/2018/jun/05/scores-of-uk-sexual-offence-cases-stopped-over-evidence-failings.

[6]   *Disclosure of Evidence in Criminal Cases*, UK Parliament (20 July 2018). Available at https://publications.parliament.uk/pa/cm201719/cmselect/cmjust/859/85903.htm#_idText Anchor000.

A spotlight was further shone on the problem when the case of *R v. Liam Allan* collapsed. The complainant in the case accused Mr. Allan of sexual assault, something he vehemently denied, saying that the sex had been consensual. The complainant's phone was analysed by the police, who determined there was no material on the phone that would assist the defence or undermine the prosecution's case. However, the downloaded phone data was not even listed as unused material.

The downloaded data was finally served, at which point text messages were found showing that the complainant had wanted and enjoyed sex with Mr. Allan.[7] The Crown realised there was no hope of a trial continuing, although it took almost *two years* to reach that point.[8]

Disclosure is absolutely core to a defence expert's chance to have a fair look at the evidence. Without it, all you are doing is reading someone else's report without the tools to evaluate its strength.

As an expert, you often have a sense of what is missing, and so can request a great deal more material, such as *all* of the scene images and CCTV footage (and not just the parts selected for the jury bundle), or *all* the phone data (and not just that selected for a prosecution timeline). To complicate things further, the defence has a right to see the information that supports the Crown's case (including the data that underpins the evidence), but the information experts may need to see is often not covered under normal disclosure rules.

In other words, we don't just need to see all the scene images, but they need to be the same full-resolution copies of the original photos so that we can zoom in and out to see more detail, not just scans or PDF versions. We need the raw CCTV footage with its bespoke player, not just

---

[7]   S. Osbourne, 'Liam Allan: Met Police Apologise to 22-Year-Old Man Falsely Accused of Rape After Failing to Disclose Crucial Text Messages', *Independent* (30 January 2018). Available at https://www.independent.co.uk/news/uk/crime/liam-allan-met-police-rape-accusation-false-evidence-disclosure-arrest-mistake-detectives-a8184916.html.

[8]   Metropolitan Police Service (MPS) and Crown Prosecution Service (CPS) London South Area, *Joint Review of the Disclosure Process in the Case of R v Allan* (30 January 2018). Available at https://www.cps.gov.uk/publication/joint-review-disclosure-process-case-r-v-allan.

an MP4 compressed file which can blur or even remove fine detail required for comparison. For DNA evidence, we need not just a summary, but the raw instrument data so that the statistics can be assessed and recalculated from scratch. For cell site analysis, we need not the police-generated tables and maps (which can contain errors), but a copy of the original Excel spreadsheets that the phone network provided, and so on.

With source data or materials, an expert can undertake a meaningful independent review of the evidence and advise the defence or the Court accordingly, without the costly and time-consuming burden of having to attend every scene or re-analyse every relevant item. This is not to say that experts never have to repeat their analysis or examine a scene in person, but usually by the time the dark side gets called, the scene has long gone and sometimes the core evidence has been altered or degraded.

Disclosure needs to be pragmatic and tempered. The criminal justice system takes no benefit from the Crown including hundreds of pages of irrelevant material in the unused material, such as detailed analytical data underpinning a drug analysis—provided there is an understanding that if a defence expert wants to see something, there are no restrictions on them doing so. It should be that easy, but I often write emails, letters or even reports explaining how the failure to allow defence experts to see exhibits or data has prevented an independent analysis and is prejudicial to the defence. In these cases it is often the judge who has to order it to be done. It wastes my time, the CPS's time, the officer-in-charge's time and, most of all, the judge's time—all for something I am entitled to see anyway.

What is interesting is how unpredictable the situation can be. Depending on the case type or jurisdiction, some police forces will be happy to send everything, sometimes without even having to ask. In other cases, it goes to a judge who might back up the prosecution's stance, leaving the defence expert only able to comment on why they couldn't check the Crown's case.

A classic example of the latter is getting the location of an automatic number plate recognition (ANPR) camera. The UK has thousands of ANPR cameras across the country continuously recording vehicle number plates. The Crown can use this data, which goes something like, "Vehicle X was recorded on ANPR on 24 October at 11:22 on the M1 in the area of Rotherham. Mobile phone evidence places the defendant's phone in the area of the vehicle at the same time as the ANPR. The evidence associates the phone with the car." That's fair enough, but it critically depends on *where* the ANPR camera in question was. The M1 around Rotherham is many miles long.

The Crown's analyst will usually produce the area that the phone was in, with a giant circle showing the location of the ANPR camera. In the most extreme case I looked at, this covered around 100 square kilometres.

Disclosure *does* allow restrictions on things that are sensitive and should not be in the public domain, an obvious example being the names of undercover officers. Yet the locations of ANPR cameras are considered by the police to be highly secret. I am not sure why: it isn't exactly MI5 material, given that if you know what road the camera is on, you can literally find it on Google Street View. For that reason, when served requests for ANPR data, some police forces will send the exact latitude and longitude of the camera, but others will insist it's top secret and cannot be revealed, even if we undertake not to put the exact location in the report.

Ultimately, if the data isn't provided, it can't be checked, and if it can't be checked, then the Crown should not be allowed to rely on it in evidence. You would think this would encourage the release of data, but I have seen several cases where the Crown ultimately just chose not to rely on the material, and a few where the judge upheld the position that the data was top secret.

There are also more subtle restrictions that have come about since the privatisation of forensic labs. The CPS and police will insist that if the defence expert wants to see data or exhibits, this has to be done at a lab nominated by the prosecution, but the lab (and also some police forces) will charge the defence to attend their facility. This places a financial barrier on the defendant getting the same access to the evidence as the Crown, which shouldn't happen.

Most cases are funded by Legal Aid, which means the cost is passed on to the public purse, but some defendants pay for their own cases. In such instances, they not only have to pay for a defence expert, but are also required to pay the Crown's expert just to have access to evidence which technically should already be covered by disclosure.

This isn't limited to examining items; the same applies to even just looking at the prosecution expert's data or case file. In one case, the police charged over £600 (US$820) for a defence expert to get a copy of the fingerprint file and photographs.

One defence solicitor was so incensed by labs charging Legal Aid for something that should ordinarily be disclosed that he took the matter to the judge, who was equally infuriated, and ordered all of the exhibits and data be sent directly to the defence expert. But cases like this are the exception and not the rule, and even worse, there are some where the police force or forensic lab get paid more Legal Aid per hour to stand around and watch me look at an exhibit than, I, as the expert, am allowed to claim for my work.

Access and disclosure are both fundamental to the equity of arms in criminal cases. As discussed throughout this book, forensic findings in isolation are rarely the issue. Rather, this lies in their meaning in the context of the wider case, and the wider case is itself often wrapped up in the unused or undisclosed material—if you get to see it. Sometimes, the first you know about it is when you turn up to court.

Expert Evidence and Court

From 1998 to 2006, the years I spent in the Cayman Islands, I was predominantly working on the side of the prosecution, but Cayman embraces change well. It was here that I first came across the true neutral role of an expert: as a servant of the court, regardless of whom you are instructed by.

I had just given evidence for the prosecution in a drug matter in Crown Court and was walking out with counsel when a well-known defence attorney on the Island walked up. He asked the prosecutor, "Do you might if I ask your expert a question about a case that is in court next week?"

Counsel shrugged and said, "Of course not. There is no ownership of experts." He paused for a moment. "But if you could let me know his answer, I'd appreciate it," he added with a wry smile.

Despite having written an alcohol analysis report for the police in a drink driving case, I was now discussing technical aspects of it directly with the defence lawyer for a trial that hadn't happened yet. As the lawyer put it, he wanted to see if he needed to advise his client to plead guilty. Counsel's words have since stuck in my head: there is no ownership of experts.

All forensic experts should be servants of the court. We all sign statements of truth and commit to professional codes of ethics, such as the International Association of Arson Investigators (IAAI's) duty to be a truth seeker and not a case-maker,[1] but it doesn't mean much if the system we work under keeps us partisan.

From around the mid-2000s, England and Wales embraced the neutrality of the expert, leading to a gradual change. By contrast, the

---

[1] See the Code of Ethics of the International Association of Arson Investigators (IAAI). Available at https://www.firearson.com/Member-Network/Code-Of-Ethics.aspx.

American legal system keeps experts very much on their respective sides. As a result, the approach to how expert evidence is presented between the US and England and Wales is very different. (Although this approach has not been formally adopted in Ireland, a Deputy Public Prosecutor's forensic expert and I were once allowed to formulate and then undertake a joint experiment together so we would both see the results. Even though we agreed on the findings, we were both asked to give, in essence, the same evidence.)

In England and Wales, it's now the norm for the court to lean on experts' independence to reduce time spent giving evidence, avoid putting complex technical arguments in front of a jury, and streamline the evidential process by having the experts meet and compile a document of points of agreement and disagreement in advance of the trial. This is true of both criminal and civil matters.

When I say that the experts meet before the trial, this can be at the courthouse literally 30 minutes before the trial starts, but if we're lucky, will be weeks or months before. It can be done in person, over the phone or by video conference, but regardless of how the discussion takes place, it normally occurs without any lawyers, barristers, colleagues or other experts present. It's usually just two or sometimes three experts (though I had one where there were four of us), talking the case through. The aim is to distil the issues into bite-sized points covering what is agreed on and what is not. (That said, more often than not, there are no points of disagreement once you've had a chance to discuss things.)

Why no points of disagreement? It comes back to what we looked at earlier: the role of context, which one or both experts may be unaware of. Armed with a fuller picture of the context, the experts can have a professional and open conversation free from prying eyes and external influences about what the evidence means. What the court therefore receives is refined forensic expertise, preferably no more than two or three pages long. If any points of disagreement remain, they are described with the reasons for and against each laid out, and it is for those points that live evidence will be given on the stand.

But before we discuss joint statements and giving evidence, we need to discuss our *reports*, because our report is the reason experts end up giving evidence. This, in turn, comes down to whether the defence or prosecution accepts them.

In the UK, forensic reports by the Crown tend to fall into two categories:

- Accepted by the defence, which happens in the majority of cases. With these, there is usually no need for the Crown's expert to attend court unless there are matters that need to be clarified.

- Not accepted by the Defence.

It is rare to get a report from a forensic lab that is plainly wrong, but this can happen for various reasons. Most of the cases where defence experts get involved are the ones where the core forensic work is correct, but the context has not been taken into consideration and so needs further interpretation.

Let's say you are a drug expert working at the request of the police, and your report states that you analysed a block of white powder which was determined to be 997g of white powder containing cocaine at 65% purity. In a case like this one, you may well not be needed for court.

If, on the other hand, the purity work wasn't done (which happens more frequently of late), or your report finds the powder contains cocaine at <5% purity, then the defence will want to know: how much less? There's a huge difference between, say, 4% purity, which is poor-quality but arguably viable cocaine, and 0.01%, which is detectable but as a trace amount. In the latter case, the white powder might be something else that has been contaminated with cocaine, but the report from the lab won't state this.

Most drug labs use ISO accredited methods. Twenty years ago, if an analyst ran a sample and found it was extremely low purity, they would tweak the sample concentration, re-run it and determine how low the purity was. That way they could advise the police on the possibility that it was a contaminated non-drug item.

These days, such a tweak will fall outside of accredited methods, so it won't get done. These methods only cover validated ranges, such as 5% to 100%; if the result is under 5%, it is simply reported as "less than 5%." The concern that the kilogram of white powder might really be contaminated material is not addressed. The officer-in-charge or police drug expert will read the result as around 5%, value it as low-purity street cocaine with a street value of over £30,000, and the suspect will be charged as a high-level drug dealer. The push to pack everything into tidy methodological boxes works for most cases, but ends up leaving some in grey areas, and others not tackled at all. Paradoxically, it falls to the defence to instruct an expert to do the investigation work.

You might think this is an extreme example, but it's not. I've worked on two cases where this happened. In both, the weighed drugs were valued at £30,000–£50,000 (US$41,000–US$68,000) a kilo, with two people facing over ten years in jail as high-level drug dealers, when the items were actually benzocaine (a non-controlled white powder) contaminated with cocaine. I worked out that the contamination in one case was about a tip of a teaspoon's worth of cocaine, spread over half a kilo of powder.

A similar issue involved a case of poisoned soup. At the prestigious Stowe public school (actually a private institution), a porter called Maxwell Cook was accused of poisoning the soup —which was going to be served to 660 students and staff—with a substance containing bleach.[2] A trainee chef, Miss Samples, said she had seen him pouring a bleach-based sanitiser from its container, like pouring from a cup of tea from a kettle, at around 3:30PM—but for reasons unknown, she didn't tell anyone.

---

[2]   'Stowe School Porter Cleared of Poisoning Soup', *BBC News* (6 April 2011) and 'Public School Porter Poured Bleach into Soup', *Mirror* (5 April 2011). Available at https://www.bbc.co.uk/news/uk-england-12986121 and https://www.mirror.co.uk/news/uk-news/public-school-porter-poured-bleach-120505.

It was the assistant chef, Mark Grace, who tasted the soup at 4:30PM, only to realise it didn't taste right and had an unpleasant smell.

Accredited forensic analysis undertaken at the request of the police found bleach in the soup, but that was all that was reported. The standard method used by the forensic laboratory detects bleach but does not give a concentration. The thing is, work *had* been done to validate the method and the controls used to make sure the instrument was running correctly, and these were enough to allow an approximate concentration to be assessed—but strict adherence to the accredited method meant it could not be reported.

The defence expert explored this with the Crown's expert. They were able to calculate the approximate volume of bleach that had been added, which was small and not what you would expect had the bleach been poured into the soup as though from a kettle. In trial, counsel for the defence accused Miss Samples of poisoning the soup to try and discredit another trainee chef.

Even in cases involving murder, the basic work isn't always done. A suspect once gave a detailed account of a murder and argued it had been self-defence, claiming he had been attacked in his own home. The murder *did* occur inside the suspect's home, and the suspect *did* have significant injuries. The normal way to resolve this kind of dispute forensically would be to look at the distribution of blood and see if it supported the version of events given.

Despite knowing this for months, with just weeks to go before trial, the police had neither commissioned a blood spatter expert to interpret the scene nor had any DNA analysed from the blood on the walls to see who it belonged to. The only reason I can think of for why this wasn't done was to save money. In the end, it was a defence expert who attended the scene and got the DNA work done as a matter of urgency.

Reports for the defence are different. They are requested because the defence either does not accept the Crown's forensic evidence, or needs forensic work to be done because the Crown hasn't done it. Either way, defence reports tend to be much more detailed and consider the case in fuller context.

Because of the differences in the way defence experts are instructed, the findings in a defence report used to fall into three categories:

- **Critical:** The defence expert's findings have a critical impact on the case and can affect its outcome. Such a report is normally served on the prosecution, leading to either the Crown deciding to drop the case (i.e. offering no evidence) or reduce the charges. If the case goes ahead, the expert will likely be asked to do a joint statement and/or testify in court.

- **Non-critical:** The analysis finds no major issues with the Crown's forensic evidence, but there are some minor ones. The defence legal team is not under any duty to serve evidence that does not assist their case, and so even if they instruct an expert report, it won't be served on the Crown if it isn't favourable. Nonetheless, it may have useful points for defence counsel to cross-examine witnesses or the Crown's expert on. The defence expert might be needed in court to listen to the Crown's expert evidence to make sure they don't go off the rails.

- **No issues:** Many review cases are prompted by the defendant not accepting the Crown's evidence. What we are asked to do in such instances is, in essence, a second opinion. It is therefore no surprise that much of the time, the original expert opinions were in agreement.

That was, at least, how it was 20 years ago. In England and Wales, we now have another category:

- **No-one read the report.** In other words, the people who needed to advise on whether the defence expert needs to attend court didn't read the report, so the expert ends up needed in court by default. On arrival, sometimes even on the way there, they may be told to go home. But because they never set foot inside the courtroom, there's a chance the court will not pay their expenses and fees.

It's sad that this last one occurs as much as it does, but it's not unexpected. Gone are the days of careful planning and pre-trial meetings weeks before the case is due to start. No more are the hour-long phone calls to discuss subtleties of your report. Before austerity, the skin was already being slowly pulled off the UK's legal system, but after the 2008 financial crash, austerity came along and went at it with a machete.

Even if the defence diligently serves an expert report weeks before a trial, the Crown Prosecution Service (CPS) or Crown barrister may not have read it (in some cases, they might not even have seen it). The default position is thus always that the expert is needed for court, even if the defence expert agrees with the Crown's own expert evidence. (If you want to read more about the England and Wales problems from a legal perspective, *The Secret Barrister* discusses issues with the current system, many of which relate to a lack of funding, in detail. It also has a great chapter on expert evidence.)[3]

There is also the rare case where the defence expert agrees with the Crown's expert evidence and thus isn't needed in court, but the trial takes a sudden and unexpected turn. This can happen when witnesses (whether they be experts or lay persons) run amok on the stand and start saying things to the jury which weren't in their statements or reports, and which may be completely outrageous.

For example, I once wrote a fire report where I agreed with the Crown's evidence. It was a relatively simple case and all of the elements pointed to it being arson. It fell to the jury to determine who committed it, but our client certainly didn't look like he was in a favourable light.

On the Friday before the trial, I had a chat with the defence solicitor, who said I wouldn't be needed at court the next week. On Monday

---

[3] Anonymous, *The Secret Barrister: Stories of the Law and How It's Broken* (Pan Books, 2019).

afternoon I got a frantic call asking if I could be at court at 10:00AM the next morning. I said the earliest I could get there would be around 10:20AM or so, as the courthouse was four and a half hours away by train from where I lived. I arrived at 10:20AM to find that court was in session, so I diligently waited outside, expecting the solicitor to arrive and tell me what was going on.

In most courtrooms, the defence expert uses the same door as the public. You enter, bow to the judge, and walk across the room to the witness stand. Not this time: this courtroom had two doors. One was the public door, which I had already glanced at, and another was a locked door that I suspected led to a janitor's closet.

Instead of the solicitor appearing, the usher came out the public entrance and said my name in that authoritarian voice all ushers have. I got ready to follow him through the public entrance, but he unlocked the janitor's closet—which turned out to be a door straight into the witness box. There I was, facing the jury like a deer in the headlights, wondering what was going on. I took the oath and away we went.

I finally met the solicitor who explained that, on Monday, the Crown's expert went rogue and started spouting all sorts of theories. This is one reason it pays to have a defence expert at a trial: had one been sitting in court the day before, it may well have kept the Crown's expert on point.

Being at Court

One major difference between expert evidence and lay witness evidence in England and Wales is that an expert's opinion is based strictly on the evidence that is said or read out in court.

When witnesses give evidence, they often add detail that wasn't present in their statements, simply because it didn't come up at the time. This may lead to further questions, and the account might change considerably from what was in their statement. However, the jury *won't* have read their statement. To them, the only account of what happened is what has been said in court, and what has been said can affect the basis of any expert's opinion. But by contrast, at that moment, you, the expert, have only read the statements, and are now unaware of the latest developments to the underlying facts of the case.

For these reasons, an expert is allowed to sit through an entire trial to hear the actual evidence presented. By this, I mean we are usually seated in the orchestra section right behind the barristers, in between the prosecution and defence lawyers.

This rarely happens in practice, due–I suspect–to time, cost, and a lack of necessity. Normally, when you give evidence, the basic facts of the case won't have materially changed since you wrote your report. This said, there *have* been a few times when I was on the witness stand, only for the barrister to start with, "I appreciate you will not know this as it wasn't in the statements you received, but yesterday in Court one of the witnesses said…".

This new information may be pitched at you without warning. At that point, you need to decide whether you can process it in a matter of seconds while standing in the spotlight, or if you should politely ask if you can have time to think about it. The court wants your answers to be right, not rushed. They should understand the situation you have been thrown in and you *can* ask for time to think about it.

What is more common is being asked to sit in while the Crown's expert gives evidence. This allows the defence to introduce you to the court at the same time as the Crown's expert, thus ensuring the Crown's expert is aware that there is another expert sitting right in front of them. If nothing else, it makes them think carefully about what they say and not start shooting from the hip. Even if they do, this can be addressed during cross-examination, with questions honed by the defence expert who has been actively listening in.

The questioning of witnesses follows the same format: direct (evidence-in-chief) from the side which has called the witness, cross-examination by the opposing side, and finally redirect (re-examination) to follow up on issues that may have come up in cross-examination. If you are sitting behind the defence barrister while the prosecution expert is giving evidence, you can whisper or pass them hurriedly scribbled notes about anything that may need to be asked, clarified or corrected.

Counsel may choose to follow up on these, but they don't always, and it's important not to take offence at this. As an expert, you tend to think your issues are critical to the case, but counsel will be looking at the bigger picture. In a typical case, the expert evidence might only be a 10–20% slice of the whole trial. Every time counsel asks a question, there is a risk of getting an answer that will harm their own case, and they therefore weigh up the risks and benefits of every question very carefully. For that reason, even if the Crown's expert says something controversial, the defence barrister might just leave it alone.

If a defence expert is going to give evidence in courts in England, Wales, Northern Ireland, and Ireland, they might be put on 'out of order': taking the stand back-to-back with the Crown's expert rather than later in the trial, when the defence is having their case heard. The idea is to have all the expert evidence heard in one go, which makes it easier for the jury to follow. This has become common practice.

Scottish courts, however, are very different in that they approach expert witnesses more like lay witnesses. You wait until you are called to give your evidence; you won't get to hear the prosecution expert's evidence or comment on it.

Back in England and Wales, beyond putting experts back-to-back, they may also be asked to take the witness stand *together*. A recent development called concurrent expert evidence, or 'hot tubbing', puts both experts in the stand at the same time so they can answer, disagree, or discuss something while standing right next to each other. The Civil Procedure Rules (CPR) formally allow this kind of evidence, as set out in Practice Direction 35.[4] Hot tubbing isn't covered in the Criminal PR, but I know of two cases where it was used in a criminal trial.

---

[4] See Civil Procedure Rules, Part 35, Practice Direction 35, paragraph 11 (Concurrent expert evidence).

Regardless of whether you think you'll have to give evidence at trial (or whether you'll need a bathing suit for it), here are a few tips for attending court:

- Take the time to plan how you will get there and if you will need to arrive the night before. Most courts will be understanding if you are late because of a horrific motorway crash or the train broke down, but not so much if you are just stuck in traffic. Similarly, plan your route to allow time for parking and walking to court (or driving, if you are coming by car, train, or flying in). I say this because all court-related staff, witnesses, family members and members of the public will try to park near the court before a session starts, and nearby parking areas will often be full before 9:00AM. If you are scheduled to go on at 10:00AM and arrive at 9:30AM, you could end up parking a 30-minute walk away.

- If you plan to read your file on the train on the way to court, be very, very careful about whether anyone can see what you are reading, and certainly don't discuss anything with anyone. You can get security visors for a laptop to keep it away from prying eyes. Other options are to get someone to pay for a first-class carriage (this might happen in the US, but generally not in the UK) or get a seat well away from others.

- If you are travelling on public transport with colleagues, be vigilant. If you make a phone call about the case, keep it anonymous and don't discuss specifics. Even if you don't mention names or places, the specifics will identify the case to anyone familiar with it. I particularly love this quote from Alexis Cleveland, whose Twitter comment appears on a brief written by barrister Gordon Exall: "I was heading to Newcastle for my first contract negotiation. Three gentlemen got on the train and sat at the same table. After eating they proceeded to discuss their strategy and bottom lines for their negotiating meeting the next day. Next morning only one of them recognised me."[5]

---

[5]   G. Exall, 'Mistakes on a Train: The Dangers of Lawyers Working on the Move', *Civil Litigation Brief* (9 April 2019). Available at https://www.civillitigationbrief.com/2019/04/09/mistakes-on-a-train-the-dangers-of-lawyers-working-on-the-move/.

- The same goes for waiting outside your courtroom. In 2021 I was sitting quietly in the corridor, and could clearly hear two police experts and the officer-in-charge discussing an issue with evidence that I had raised.

- Get to court early and scope out the courtroom before it sits. There is normally an opportunity when the court is unlocked and the place is empty save for the Clerk. Knowing the layout makes it easier when you go in later, and removes anxiety about walking in with no idea where you are going (which the jury may well pick up on).

Once, in a court in Northern Ireland, I was asked to go into the dock to be ready. Thankfully, neither the judge nor the jury were sitting as I looked around at the walls of wood with no idea where to go. It turned out I had to walk up two staircases into the dock, which was set high up along with the judge and jury; the barristers were in a pit below me. Another time, in Ireland, I had to give evidence at Nenagh District Court. I got there about 9:30AM and went through the front door to find no security, reception or anyone else present. I found my courtroom and, finding the door to be unlocked, popped my head in to see if anyone was inside. The courtroom was completely empty, but all of the exhibits were out on display. At this point, I quietly did a U-turn and went to wait in the main entrance.

- If the Clerk is there and the court is not sitting, let the Clerk know who you are and why you are there. They may have you already on their list.

- Bring two spare copies of your report. In England and Wales, there's a chance you may have to have a conference with your counterpart, who might not have seen your report until that very moment.

- Bring loose sheets of paper or sticky notes in case you need to pass notes to the barrister. No one wants to hear you trying to slowly tear off a piece of paper in a hushed courtroom.

- Bring a hard copy or laptop containing all the material you relied upon, including your instructions if you relied upon them in writing your report (which most experts will have). In a criminal trial, everything in your report (including your instructions) is technically disclosable, and in one trial I was asked to produce them. I think the opposing counsel was just trying to rattle me, but it backfired when I handed them over.

- By bringing all the material you relied upon, you can also demonstrate, if needed, whether any of it differs from what is in the jury bundle. I've arrived at court more than once to a set of photos I'd never seen. One of these was a murder case, and it required a halt to the trial for me to review them (which resulted in me changing my opinion).

- When it comes to photos, notes and other material on your laptop, a lot of courtrooms now have a system where they can put a dongle in your laptop that will share your screen to the court monitors. That way, you can refer to photos easily and it's a lot better than being passed a pair of scissors by the Clerk so you can cut a photo out of your report to hand to a jury! The only thing to make sure is that there's nothing distasteful on your laptop screen or wallpaper, in case everyone happens to see it.

Coming to give testimony is another matter. What you thought you came to discuss and how you thought you would do that can be negated by what happened when you weren't present in court the day before. As an expert for the defence, for all your preparations, you also have to accept:

- You may be walking into a court (and sometimes in a country) in which you have never given evidence in before.

- You may not have the benefit of a conference with counsel beforehand, especially if it's a criminal matter in the UK.

- You might not even be asked anything about what you prepared for.

Fundamentally, you have to remember your role in any given case. You are not there to make a jury decide one thing or another; you are there to provide further information as an expert. You will be giving evidence about events at which you were not present. Your opinion may be right or wrong, but regardless of what you feel about it, the jury will be balancing it against other evidence, witness accounts and propositions, including those of opposing experts.

The jury will have been sitting days or weeks listening to evidence before they hear you. The prosecution will be trying to convince them of the Crown's case; the defence will be trying to undermine the Crown's case and/or convince them of their own. Dialogue is semi-scripted, as counsel for either party will have decided ahead of time which witnesses need to appear to be questioned (as opposed to having their statements read out). They will have a list of questions to ask, ones they hope they already know the answer to.

You, as an expert, might know in your heart you are correct, but ultimately it doesn't mean much if you aren't able to engage the jury. If they don't get it or don't listen, all that expert work will be wasted or lost in the days and weeks of other voices they will go on to hear. This is why your ability to hold a jury's attention, and speak clearly in a way that people can understand, is core to being a good expert.

You are going to be questioned by two parties: the ones who instructed you (direct questioning) and the opposing side (cross-examination). *Leading the witness* is a common style of questioning in dealing with experts, where you are asked 'yes or no'-type questions. Barristers prefer this as it keeps their questions focused, gets them the answers they want for summing up, and minimises the risk of an expert babbling on and opening up a can of worms by accident.

There's nothing wrong with a leading approach unless the answer isn't yes or no. "Did you go to the scene on 2nd March?" is usually a yes or no question. On the other hand, "Would you agree that the blood on the knife matches the defendant?" may have a level of support such that the answer isn't a straight yes or no, but something like, "I think there's extremely strong support the blood has come from the defendant."

There is a common assumption that the other side will be out to get you, but in my experience, this is rarely the case. Both sides want to get the expert to make admissions for their case that they can use in summing up for the jury. For example, in a trace DNA case, the Crown will want the expert to say that Mr. X's DNA was present on item Y. The defence will want to discuss the statistic behind this and how weak the evidence pointing to their client is, or whether it could have arrived there from somewhere else.

A barrister would rather get certain admissions from you without a fight. Any time they try to bully or discredit an expert, there is a risk it will backfire, especially if they haven't done their research well.

> **Q:** Dr. Schudel, would you agree that an understanding of mobile phones is important to this case?
>
> **A:** Yes, I agree.
>
> **Q:** And would you agree that there is nothing in your experience as to any formal qualifications or expertise in mobile phones?
>
> **A:** There isn't, Counsel, but I was a forensic phone examiner for five years and produced 500 reports on them, though I now realise this wasn't on my CV.

If counsel decides to bully you, there are three common outcomes: remaining stoic, becoming argumentative or defensive, or crumbling in the box. You might think this an oft-used tactic, but in reality, no one likes a bully. If you don't react and counsel continues to bully you, or you crumble (and I know a few cases where this happened), the jury may well take pity on you and cause the strategy to backfire.

Where it *does* work is when an expert starts to get into an argument with counsel or seems to be overly defensive. At this point, the jury will start to wonder why they are arguing (are they hiding something?) and the expert starts to lose credibility.

How you answer and react to those first few questions may affect the tactic a barrister will take. Take this example on cross-examination with a choice of two responses, the first being neutral and the second being defensive, and see how you feel about my responses:

> **Q:** Dr. Schudel, would you say that this is not a common area of forensics?
>
> **A:** No, it is not.
>
> vs.
>
> **Q:** Dr. Schudel, would you say that this is not a common area of forensics?
>
> **A:** I'm not sure what you mean?

Or this example:

> **Q:** This isn't an area you would normally find people who are experts.
>
> **A:** Yes, Counsel, it's very much a niche.
>
> vs.
>
> **Q:** This isn't an area you would normally find people who are experts.
>
> **A:** I think you'll find there *are* experts, and I *am* one of them.

Sometimes you will get statements put to you without any question accompanying it. At others, you will get a string of questions all in one paragraph (i.e. stacked questions). Counsel might be doing it deliberately to confuse or alienate you. There is nothing wrong with asking what the question is, or whether they could break them down one at a time. The judge will invariably step in if things get too confusing, as if the expert is lost, then the jury likely is too.

With stacked questions, make a mental note of the number of questions asked so that after you have answered the one that you can remember, you can ask counsel to repeat the others.

'No-question questions' are tricky. They sound like questions, and you can answer them as if they were, but make sure you caveat any uncertainties rather than being drawn down a path that you aren't comfortable with.

Let's take an example of a case involving a fight between Mr. Smith and Mr. Jones. Blood was spilt, but DNA analysis has not been done on some of the stains, and it is not clear who the blood belongs to. Counsel might state, "These stains of blood here and here are Mr. Smith's, and these ones here from Mr. Jones'."

No question has been asked. If you say yes, it will sound like you agree with whose blood made the stains, but as DNA analysis wasn't done, factually, you don't know this. Do you wait (as no question was asked)? Do you ask counsel what their question is? Or do you respond as if it was a question but caveat your answer, such as, "I noted those are blood stains but DNA hasn't been on those ones so I can't say which person they came from?"

If your evidence doesn't provide any points that counsel would like to use in their summing up, they may decide that the only course of action is to try and discredit your opinion. There are various ways of doing this:

- Looking for areas where you may have overstated your qualifications, such people adding post-nominals when the organisation involved doesn't allow this. In the days of the former Forensic Science Society, some experts put MFSS (Member of the Forensic Science Society) after their name, even though the society had no professional membership status.

- Undermining your qualifications, particularly those where you only need to pay an annual fee and do some annual or other periodic testing to maintain. Similarly, if there is a common qualification that experts in this field tend to have and you don't, they might ask why you haven't got it.

- Pointing out that you haven't published any papers or articles.

- Reviewing your training to see when you last did any relevant to this case.

- Bringing up articles, blogs, or website postings where you appear to show a different opinion on the same subject, or have displayed sexism, racism or other bias that may have a bearing on the case.

- Bringing up any disciplinary actions or cases where your evidence or report was not accepted by a court.

- Demonstrating that publications or information you have relied upon in your report are irrelevant or unreliable.

- Making you look out of touch. An easy example of this is experts who don't keep up with the changes in wording for the Declarations of Truth required by an expert in their report. In one 2021 case, a report from an expert had an ISO quality management logo on it, but a declaration in its text referred to Part 33 of the Criminal Procedure Rules on the duties of experts–which had been changed in 2015 to Part 19.

- Trying to undermine the basis of the opinion. For example, if the expert is very much reliant on an eyewitness account, then they might explore the weaknesses in eyewitness evidence or any discrepancies between the eyewitness accounts.

- Pointing out instances where the expert seems to have ignored something that contradicts their opinion.

If you think any of these things might have a bearing on your testimony, then you need to have answers for them. If you, like most people working in a large forensic laboratory, haven't done any external training for over five years, then you need to at least provide a reason for this and why you feel it poses no issues.

As for the rest, don't rise to any debate. If you can't answer the question, say you can't answer, but always do so calmly and to the jury. If counsel persists, then stick with your answer.

In one case, the barrister basically kept asking me the same question over and over, which I answered the same way each time. The judge finally told him to move on as the question had been asked and answered, but counsel insisted on having another go. This time, I didn't answer straight away, but paused and waited for the judge to intervene.

When a judge intervenes, it can go one of two ways: they will either look at you with that 'please continue' face, or they will look at counsel to tell them something, which is what happened in this instance.

"Counsel," said the judge sternly, "Once again, the witness has been asked and has answered this question."

The barrister replied, "Your Honour, I don't believe the witness has given an answer."

"Yes, he has. It's just not the answer you want. Now move along."

Here are some basics to adopt when giving evidence; they help keep things from getting ugly. None of them come from a course or a book.

Rather, they are things I have learned and have seen others do well or badly.

1. Before you even set foot in court to testify or listen to evidence, check that your mobile is OFF and your laptop speakers are OFF. Check that your clothing is not dishevelled, and your laces, zips, and buttons are done up as they should be.

2. Take only what you need. If you have baggage (for example, if you are staying overnight), ask the court usher where to put it before you enter.

3. When listening to others' evidence in court, do so intently, take notes, and do not make any noises, sounds or expressions that show you agree or disagree with what is being said. Not only is it unprofessional: if the judge catches it, he or she will ask the jury to step out before—rightly—telling you off.

4. Arrive in the witness stand like a professional. The jury have likely been told they will be hearing expert evidence. If they are already sitting when you enter, you want them to watch in awe as you glide calmly across the court without tripping over your laces or dropping your books and notes. Only take what you need, and have it organised so you can lay it out in the dock as you arrive (except in Scotland, where you aren't allowed to refer to your notes this way).

5. Should you sit or stand? In Northern Ireland and Ireland (though it happened to me for the first time in England in 2021—might be my grey hairs), courts will often invite you to sit down. Some experts choose to stand; I generally sit down, but you may want to think about your choice beforehand in case you are asked. Whatever you do, keep your posture upright, shoulders dropped and chin up. Look bright and alert like a meerkat. If you have a physical reason why you cannot stand, like a bad back, let the usher know in advance.

6. For goodness' sake, don't mumble. I have seen experts be reminded numerous times to raise their voices. One reminder is fair enough; after the second one, the jury might just start to think you're an idiot. If they can't hear you, they will switch off.

7. That said, if you see a microphone, you might have to moderate your volume. If needed, adjust the microphone so it is close by while you are standing or sitting, then speak clearly and loudly. If, at that point, you can hear your words echoing off the far side of the courtroom, apologise to the jury and speak more quietly. (Yes, I have done this.)

   Another issue is that some microphones are highly directional, such that if you move a few centimetres to one side it won't pick up your voice, but when you raise your voice in response and move back towards the microphone, you sound like you are screaming. If, like me, you find it hard to stay still when talking, I just move away from the microphone and speak loudly so I know the jury can hear me regardless.

8. Listen to the question but talk to the jury. I can't stress this enough. Look at who is asking the question and listen, then pause, look at the jury, and give your answer. I have seen seasoned experts make the mistake of ending up in an eye-to-eye conversation with the barrister, at which point the jury starts to feel they are being left out and the credibility of your testimony starts to diminish.

9. Another classic tactic in cross-examination is trying to break your rapport with a jury. Counsel will start asking a question while walking across the courtroom, *away* from the jury. The idea is to make you turn your head away from them in the hope you will answer looking at the barrister and not the jury. It's easy to counter this: after they ask the question, pause, turn your head back and talk to the jury.

10. Always pause after a question is asked, whether on direct or cross-examination. There are a few reasons for this. One is that you set

the pace of the testimony. Counsel might speed up to try and pressure you into giving an answer that they want, but perhaps is not what you mean to say. Take a pause each time to break that cycle.

Another reason is to create a similar rhythm, whether you are being questioned direct or on cross-examination. Experts often engage in what seems to be an almost rehearsed manner in direct, but get hostile and awkward on cross-examination. I've watched them do it. If you pause after all questions, it tends to set a similar rhythm for both, and that helps give a sense of neutrality. Finally, a pause gives a moment for either the other side or the judge to object to the question.

11. Answer calmly at an appropriate volume. Keep the same tenor when you are talking. Don't get defensive or raise your voice. I am quite animated when giving evidence, so I tend to wave my arms around. (I think it helps to keep everyone's attention, but it might just annoy them. I've never asked.)

12. Treat direct and cross-examination as the same thing. In most cases, something you have said or know will favour the other side; it's inevitable. Counsel, on cross-examination, will want to get that on the record.

For example, if a fingerprint could have been left on a knife prior to the incident, such as when the defendant bought it at the shop, counsel for the defence will want to make this seem like the explanation for how the fingerprint got on the knife. On cross-examination, counsel for the prosecution will want you to agree that the fingerprint could also have been left on the knife by the defendant being at the incident. The answer to that is, "Yes, that could also explain it." No long pauses, ifs or buts. You are an expert for the court, so just answer the question, and if you don't know, then just say, "I don't know."

I have seen experts give good, coherent evidence on direct, but start to squirm, get combative, lean forward, or perspire on cross-examination. If your demeanour changes or you start to get combative when answering a question that favours the other side, that makes you look biased or as though you're hiding something. The jury will pick up on the change in your manner, as will counsel, who will then pursue it to make you look even worse. On my part, I try to think that both sides are out to get me but one side doesn't realise it, and that helps keep my demeanour consistent between them.

13. Use analogies. A judge once explained circumstantial evidence to a jury with this analogy: "If I found that half the chocolate in the jar in the kitchen cupboard seemed to be missing, and my grand-daughter was in the lounge with chocolate around her mouth, I might not have the chocolate jar seized from her hand as evidence, but you (the jury) could be invited consider the matter using cir-cumstantial evidence instead." It was a perfect analogy that got a smile from the courtroom.

Analogies are powerful tools for reducing complex issues into things that people might understand. Gas chromatography can be com-pared to the school experiment where a dot of black ink was placed on a piece of paper, and separated into different colours when a liquid was added. Mass spectrometry can be likened to knowing which exact Lego set you bought by the range and numbers of pieces you counted from the bag. Cell sites and cells can be compared to lighthouses and their beams of light. The retention of gunshot residue on hands is a bit like picking up tiny ball bearings. And so on. You have to be able to do this or no one will understand you.

Before you give evidence, think about what analogies might be useful. Try explaining them to non-experts to see if they get the idea.

Overall, I have had very few rough days in court, and only twice where I have been openly roasted. One of these was in Scotland. where the sheriff basically accused me of being a 'bought expert' who had been told what to do by the defendant's solicitor. I explained how I had made my own decisions about how to reconstruct the events and the testing I did, but he persisted. Had I been ten years younger, I might have crumbled, but at that point in my career I told him that I didn't like the tone of his questions, that I had not been coerced into my findings, and that if the prosecution were really concerned about what I had done, they had ample opportunity to go and repeat the work themselves.

It was brave, but you can't let some things pass. As much as you must respect the court, the court also needs to respect you. Anyone who questions your neutrality on record, without any evidence, is acting in a reckless fashion. If you don't defend yourself, you run the risk of destroying your career.

Ethical Issues

As much as you might consider yourself as an independent expert in service of the court, it's not always that easy. In both the UK and US, the defence has no obligation to serve any material which under-mines their case. At the simplest level, this means if I (as the defence expert) write a report that agrees with the Crown, the defence just won't serve it.

If I write a report that agrees on some major issues but takes issue with minor ones, the defence might use my report to cross-examine the Crown's expert and try and unseat them, but they still won't serve my report.

There are cases, however, where the evidence does not support the defendant's account—only for the defendant, after catching sight of the report, to suddenly recall what they were doing that night. Lo and behold, the story fits, and the defence then asks you to amend your report with your new instructions.

What do you do?

1. You can do as requested and pretend the first report doesn't exist. This will score maximum customer service points and no one will

know—unless the Crown somehow finds out (for example, if a copy of the first report was accidentally sent to the CPS). If this happens, you can kiss your career goodbye. This is *not* the ethical option, though I imagine there are experts out there who would take the risk.

2. You could refuse, but the problem with this is the defendant might actually be telling the truth, and by refusing, you are now doing more harm than good.

3. Ethically, you make the amendment as requested, but clearly state that this is an amended version of your previous report, following receipt of further instructions (explaining what these are). You meet the request to do the work while making it transparent.

As you might expect, some clients will be upset by the third approach, but this is business you don't need. Never put your reputation on the line for one client.

Sadly, one consequence of this I have seen in 'hip-flask' defence (drink driving) cases is that the solicitor takes your report, uses it to work out what their client should have consumed for a post-driving defence, and instructs a different expert with that information.

This does happen in major cases too, including a murder where I had managed to not only agree with the Crown but made their case water-tight. The defendant, who had financial means, sacked his entire legal and expert team and started again with a new one. I only found out when my replacement and I attended a conference together and he happened to mention an odd case he had worked on. Thankfully, we came to the same opinion via different pathways (and the defendant was found guilty of murder).

There is sometimes a middle ground in these cases, which falls between your role as an expert and your duty to the court. An example might go like this: you are given specific instructions by counsel to look at the provenance of five images relating to an alleged rape of a young woman (the complainant) by a young man (the defendant). The complainant says she was raped by him and he took photos, but the defendant says they were in a consensual relationship and she had emailed the photos to him. During your examination, you find 100 other compromising images of the complainant. What do you do?

We experts are very much bound by our instructions. You were asked to comment on five photos, which is all the Crown is presenting as evidence. There is no legal duty or obligation for the defence to present any more evidence than that.

However, should you mention the extra 100 photos or not? If all of them had been sent by the complainant to the defendant, this would seem to exonerate the defendant and support his account. However, if all hundred of them, plus the extra five, were taken on the defendant's phone, then the case is far worse than it first appeared, but the Crown has missed this key evidence.

Ethically, I would argue that you should put them in, regardless of which account of events they favour. Legally, however, if they don't favour the defendant's case, then counsel will come back to your instructions and ask why you didn't follow them, since you are obliged to report only on what you were asked to do. My usual response to this would be that if I have managed to figure something out, there's a chance the prosecution's expert will do the same, and we would end up in the same situation regardless. (At one point, there were rumours that the law might be changed such that any defence expert report which had been requested would need to be served, but it's been a few years and nothing came of it.)

A similar issue can happen on the witness stand in cases where your report favours the defence overall, but there is support for the Crown's account of events. In such cases, you might find that counsel for the defence will put you on the stand and only ask about the parts of your report which help their client. Cross-examination will present a chance to pick up on the points that help the Crown's case, but if the prosecutor forgets to ask about them, is it your place to interrupt the trial to offer evidence you weren't asked about?

Voir Dire or Grand Jury Hearings

Although rare, a *voir dire* (UK) or grand jury (US) hearing is a means to check the admissibility of evidence before it goes before a real jury. They are slightly different in that in the UK, the *voir dire* has no jury and the evidence is heard by the judge in a mock trial. A grand jury hearing, by comparison, involves up to 23 jurors who listen to the key parts of the evidence and decide if there is enough to go on for a fair trial. In my 30 years of experience, I have attended only one of each.

The grand jury hearing took place when I was based in Massachusetts. The case of *Commonwealth v. Jada Amicone and Michael Panagopoulos* was brought after Amicone's two children, aged three and five, died in a fire. The charges were brought after it turned out that the bedroom door had been locked from the outside so the children couldn't get out. It followed that one of the children must have had a lighter or match inside the bedroom.

The jury found the pair guilty of assault, but were split on whether Amicone was guilty of manslaughter.[6] Prior to any case being brought, it went to grand jury to see if there was sufficient evidence to charge her with.

Grand jury is very different from court. Rather than taking the stand and being led by seasoned legal practitioners to give evidence, it's more akin to giving a presentation onstage to an audience, after which they (the jury) will put up their hands and ask you questions.

In many ways, I wish regular court was like this, as it was refreshingly open and far less stressful—with the one exception that someone paged

---

[6] H.B. Perman, 'Split Verdict in Mass. Trial', *AP News* (27 May 2000). Available at https://apnews.com/article/db144937321c162373527bee722afc79.

me from work in the middle of it. Having been called from work to attend, it hadn't occurred to me that anyone would page me; no-one calls me during work hours because I'm *at work*. Naturally, I got paged about an hour into giving my evidence with the pager on vibrate and tucked onto my belt.

Giving evidence is intense regardless of which court you are in, but when the pager suddenly vibrated against my waist, I froze and my eyes went wide as though I'd just been given an electric shock. I can still see the alarmed faces of the grand jury, who must have wondered what had happened to me. (As I mentioned: always make sure your phone, pager, smart watch, or what have you is *switched off*.)

By comparison, a *voir dire* hearing runs more or less formally like a trial. I say more or less as there is no jury sitting, so the flow and pattern of questions is less tense.

The case in question involved a jealous boyfriend. He was alleged to have poured a flammable liquid into the letter-box of his ex-girlfriend's house and set fire to it. An unusual flammable liquid had been detected on the floor inside the house and on his clothing. You would think this was pretty good evidence—except that the same chemical could also have come about from contamination of the bags used to collect the evidence.

In flammable liquid cases, it's good practice to always include an empty 'control' bag as part of the evidence, so that the lab can check to make sure the bags are not contaminated before being used. It sounds like a rare occurrence, but contaminated bags crop up from time to time, and the fact that the flammable liquid detected was uncommon made the risk of contamination more likely. (It also didn't help that the supplier of these bags turned out to be a one-man business based out of a garage. Who knows how the bags had been stored prior to being shipped to the police's stores?)

The Crown's evidence wasn't helped by the crime scene investigator, who, when asked why a control bag hadn't been included, said that it wasn't part of their training. This was a revelation, as the existing training material and the Crown's forensic scientist said control bags *were* required—though he went on to say that often they weren't included. He agreed that the results could be due to contamination of the bag.

We all ended up giving evidence over the course of a day in what felt like a mock trial. In the end, the judge felt that while the bags could have been contaminated prior to use, the issue should be brought before a jury to decide. We showed up again the week after for the real trial, although, as the Crown's barrister said to me, at least we all knew what we were going to say.

This time round, there was plenty of witness and circumstantial evidence to support the case, which probably could have been run without any forensics. I suspect this was the reason why the judge allowed the trial to go ahead.

The Future: It's Not What It Used to Be

There is a tendency for humans to think that something can be done as long as we can imagine it. This is not true. The laws of physics dictate what we can or can't do. Much as we have made certain inroads into understanding the physical limitations of our universe, just because we still don't fully comprehend certain things doesn't mean they are possible.

Time travel, for example, is a common theme in science fiction, including using it to solve murders which took place in the past. In reality, time travel either exists or it doesn't. Time can either be traversed or it can't: if time only exists as a discrete moment, then it has no past or future, and time travel will never happen. That said, even if it doesn't exist, humans will likely still spend a thousand years trying to unlock its secrets, simply because there is no way to prove otherwise.

Around 10,000–12,000 BCE, the agricultural revolution turned hunter-gatherers into farmers and changed the core ways in which humans formed groups, lived, and interacted with each other. This led to the development of larger societies, and by 0 BCE, cities with complex laws had sprung up.

Over the 18ᵗʰ and 19ᵗʰ centuries, the Industrial Revolution saw a prolific rise in machines and technology, which allowed humans to evolve at a massively increased rate. Within 200 years of that, we had landed on the moon.

With the invention of societies also came the adoption of laws. Law and order are often taken to be the same thing, but they are not. Law is what society demands; order is what happens, in theory, if people follow the law. Almost all societies have laws, but successful societies are generally those which have fair and reasonable laws *and* abide by them—i.e. they have a measure of order.

Having order makes it much easier for those who are charged with upholding the law to focus on the few who do not follow it and act accordingly, whether by intervention, education, rehabilitation or punishment. Things fall apart when so many people fail to act in an orderly fashion that the rule of law breaks down. That society might have laws, but it generally will not evolve without some semblance of order.

Some laws are reasonably self-explanatory, such as a prohibition on committing murder. Others are born out of the needs of society at a particular time.

To ensure England had enough trained archers to combat invaders, Henry VIII enacted legislation requiring men under the age of 40 to bear bows and arrows.[1] The requirement ran for centuries before being removed from the statute books, but at the time it was decreed, it made sense.

Historically, salt was considered to be highly valuable, so stealing it was considered a serious crime. Had current forensic techniques been available thousands of years ago, we would doubtless have one for chemically fingerprinting salt so as to be able to track the source from which it came, and to look for traces of it on a person's clothing.

Currency has been the cornerstone of societies for thousands of years. Since the 20th century, there has been a shift towards fiat currency, which are government-issued legal tender, but in itself consists of pieces of paper with numbers written on them—what we assign value to as money.

Despite fiat currency having no material value, entire and numerous legal structures have been built around its use, backed by forensic techniques from fingerprinting, DNA, drug detection, counterfeit detection, and digital analysis through to forensic accounting.

---

[1] K. Underhill, 'Do Englishmen Still Have to Show up for Longbow Practice?', *Lowering the Bar* (24 June 2010). Available at https://loweringthebar.net/2010/06/do-englishmen-still-have-to-show-up-for-longbow-practice.html.

Crimes associated with these are deemed very serious indeed. The penalty for fraud can be up to ten years in prison, which is comparable to what someone might receive for manslaughter.[2] A large-scale fraud can drastically affect the lives of thousands of people; even though someone might not have died as a direct result of the fraud, its impact can be severe enough to warrant serious punishment for those who perpetrate such a crime.

We have seen how laws have evolved in response to societies' needs just recently, with the enactment of various laws designed to control the spread of COVID-19 in the UK. These laws included heavy fines or imprisonment for congregating or going on holiday. Forensic techniques may have to be developed to determine whether someone has been vaccinated, and whether their paperwork is fraudulent.

The future of forensics will track the same philosophy: as societies' needs change, so will their laws and so will the forensic methods to go with them. Much will depend on what our future looks like, and there are some worryingly obvious issues to consider: climate change and raw materials.

There will come a time when oil runs low and becomes highly valuable. Since many plastics are manufactured using oil, the price of plastic will soar. As oil stocks dwindle, society may turn to landfill mining to recover discarded non-biodegradable plastics. If this happens, penalties for theft and fraud of plastic may become severe. Forensic science methods will be developed to chemically fingerprint plastics and residues on plastics to landfill signatures, and then connect stolen plastics to specific landfills. All of this for the same plastic that, right now, some people toss out of a car window.

---

[2] See the Sentencing Guidelines for Fraud, Bribery and Money Laundering Offences (effective from 1 October 2014) and Unlawful Act Manslaughter (effective from 1 November 2018), UK Sentencing Council. Available at https://www.sentencingcouncil.org.uk/sentencing-and-the-council/about-sentencing-guidelines/about-published-guidelines/fraud-bribery-and-money-laundering/ and https://www.sentencingcouncil.org.uk/offences/crown-court/item/unlawful-act-manslaughter/.

Each human consumes oxygen and exhales carbon dioxide as a result of breathing and digestion. The meat that humans consume also comes from animals that do the same. Transporting food requires fuel, which creates carbon dioxide as a by-product. As population growth increases, carbon dioxide emissions will rise from a combination of all of these factors.

But people take up space, and our carbon footprints aren't exactly proportionate to this. How many trees are lopped down to make space for houses? How many gardens are built over and turned into car parks? As the population keeps expanding, the amount of land available to grow plants (that reduce carbon dioxide) shrinks. This cycle will inevitably continue until crisis takes hold.

At some point, laws may be enacted, possibly by worldwide agreement, to urgently reverse the problem. Crimes against the environment will carry heavier and heavier penalties. Having a bonfire could be a serious crime. Smoking may be banned worldwide. Beef could be outlawed. Forensic techniques will have to adapt to these new laws to track down offenders and the anticipated black market that will accompany regulation. These could involve the use of a network of drone or remote smoke sensors to track and report any spikes in carbon dioxide levels.

On the flip side of the same crisis, population control (possibly akin to the one-child policy enforced in China in the 1970s and 1980s) may become a globally agreed requirement, out of the desperate need to rebalance the world. This could spark an entire underground network of human trafficking which will need forensic methods to combat.

This might seem like the result of an overactive imagination, or perhaps the stuff of science fiction, but 2,000 years ago, a Roman would have gasped in shock to learn that salt would one day be a throwaway commodity.

There is also the next revolution to consider. The agricultural revolution was followed by the Industrial Revolution. In the future, there will be AI: the artificial intelligence revolution.

We're nowhere near it at present. AI requires some form of intelligence behind processing beyond just the juggling of large amounts of data. The fact that I can buy a spare tyre off a website and then be bombarded with adverts on different websites for—you've guessed it—*another* spare tyre shows how poorly developed the current AI systems are. The AI that the media keeps talking about doesn't exist, and the programmes and software we have still need massive amounts of human supervision to keep them from dropping off the silicon highway.

But AI is coming. We are building bigger and faster computers, capturing masses of raw data, and processing hugely complex algorithms in a way that humans are unable to do. Already, facial recognition systems can spot faces and track a crowd of people with an alarming degree of accuracy; marketing giants can predict your likes by analysing your online behaviour. When AI kicks in, this will be child's play, but I suspect the role of the defence expert will be the same: the facts are often right, but context changes its interpretation. If the AI doesn't have the full context, then it will produce the same issues that we see right now.

Given the rapid advances that technology is experiencing, there are some obvious forensic advances ahead.

DNA analysis has moved along in leaps and bounds, especially the sequencing of the human genome—a project which took 13 years to complete.[3] Since then, forensic DNA has already started to look at reverse-engineering individual traits such as eye and hair colour.[4] It doesn't take too huge a leap to imagine how more and more traits could eventually be calculated from a sample found at a crime scene. One day, traces from a crime scene will be reverse engineered into an actual 3-D image of what that person should look like. And as with any leap in

---

[3] See the National Human Genome Research Institute website. Available at https://www.genome.gov/human-genome-project.

[4] S. Walsh et al., 'The HIrisPlex System for Simultaneous Prediction of Hair and Eye Colour from DNA', *Forensic Science International: Genetics* (7) 9–115 (2013). Available at https://doi.org/10.1016/j.fsigen.2012.07.005.

forensic technology, a countering response, such as DNA modification and plastic surgery to alter appearances, will follow.

For many years, I wondered about the use of smell. Currently, dogs can be used to pick up a scent and follow it from a crime scene to a suspect's house. However, leads often go cold, and even a good lead can't be established in evidence. But if a dog can detect a scent and single it out from all the others, then in theory, we should be able to make an analytical device that could do the same. Scene profiling would be as specific and unique as DNA profiling, with the added advantage of being able to isolate and track a scent. One day we will end up running around the streets with a box that can analyse scent (or mount it on a drone instead).

Scene processing will see a change from humans to AI-controlled devices. We already have high-resolution laser-mapping that can produce incredibly defined scene images, including the size and shape of blood stains and bullet trajectory for analysis.[5] The main obstacle to their widespread rollout is cost, but that will drop in time. Rapid DNA technology is already being researched and touted as the next tool in the crime scene investigator (CSI's) arsenal, which would allow CSIs to get preliminary DNA results in minutes—perhaps while they are still at the crime scene.[6]

With an AI core, robotics, and small-scale DNA and chemical analysis (types of which are already being used on the Mars rovers), a CSI lab system should theoretically be able to dynamically map a scene whilst checking for and analysing trace evidence (hairs, fibres, glass, foreign particles, DNA, and so on). The AI would discount common ones and capture relevant ones in real time. Whilst working, the drone smell analyser I was talking about would lift off and start tracking foreign scents.

---

[5]   See, for example, the services provided by FARO at https://www.faro.com/en-gb/application/crime-scene-analysis-2/.

[6]   A.A. Mapes et al., 'Decision Support for Using Mobile Rapid DNA Analysis at the Crime Scene', *Science & Justice* 59(1) 29–45 (2019). Available at https://doi.org/10.1016/j.scijus.2018.05.003.

Such a lab might still be a few decades away, but features of such methods are already in development. Rapid scene DNA is becoming more widespread; in the US, the Federal Bureau of Investigation (FBI) has already approved its use for searching reference standards against their national offender database without manual interpretation and review.[7] In time, this will grow into scene work. Low quantities and mixtures of substances might continue to present limitations, but for scenes where there are blood, saliva or other single bodily fluids, the police will be generating leads from DNA in minutes rather than days. Issues might arise with things like blood mixtures, where interpretation would still be needed, but non-reference samples should always have some degree of overview if they are used to identify a suspect.

Human traces like sweat and unusable fingerprints can already be sampled for toxicology profiles,[8] which can help in assessing the accounts of events given by suspects. Imagine this expanding to other markers found in sweat that are characteristic of individuals, including specific hormones, nutrient profiles and biochemical patterns. Someone who takes a specific supplement each day might be linked to a crime by the profile of vitamins and minerals in their sweat, and so even the shopping habits of a suspect could become evidence in the case.

But academia and the real world of forensics are driven by very different engines. Going back a few decades, there was a time in the UK when you could do things like figure out what car was involved in a hit-and-run by matching paint taken from a victim to a database of cars. Fibres and glass from suspects' clothing and scenes were often compared against general background levels, and ongoing studies of these background levels of various trace types in various settings would be carried out year on year. Over the last decade, reduced demand means such lab analyses

---

[7] 'FBI Approves Thermo Fisher Scientific's Rapid DNA Solution for National DNA Index System', *ThermoFisher Scientific* (8 September 2020). Available at https://www.thermofisher.com/blog/behindthebench/fbi-approves-thermo-fisher-scientifics-rapid-dna-solution-for-national-dna-index-system/.

[8] See, for example, M. Hudson et al., 'Drug Screening Using the Sweat of a Fingerprint: Lateral Flow Detection of Δ9-Tetrahydrocannabinol, Cocaine, Opiates and Amphetamine', *Journal of Analytical Toxicology* 43(2) 88–95 (2019). Available at https://doi.org/10.1093/jat/bky068.

have been pared back to a skeleton of their former selves. The less they are used, the more expensive they are to maintain, and the smaller they become.

Alongside the overall reduction in forensic service, a critical eye was cast over several currently accepted forensic methods, such as the world of fingerprint comparisons. Despite over a century of comparisons—all of which, ostensibly, leave no room for doubt about who might have left a fingermark—validation studies have been trickling out demonstrating the weakness in this system, which is used the world over. The risk of false positives in close non-matching (CNM) marks has recently been demonstrated in a joint study conducted by the US and China, which found a staggering average false positive rate of 15.9% in a proficiency study that included two CNMs sent to 125 participating agencies.[9] Further studies will erode confidence in the current comparison system and force change—whatever that might entail.

One approach might be to treat fingerprint comparison to statistical modelling more akin to DNA, based on the type of mark and the matching characteristics. This would allow for a representation of the evidence that reflects its strength, but it is a huge culture change, and statistics is an area of expertise not shared by everyone.

Since most private forensic lab spending comes out of the police budget, I suspect there will continue to be a preference for the police to minimise what they spend externally and focus on doing forensic work in-house, as opposed to sending it out to private labs. At the moment, fingerprints and digital forensics are typically done in-house, but some police forces have drug analysis facilities, and I anticipate they will look to more sophisticated technologies in the future to save money. Lancashire police, for example, are already looking at a joint enterprise with four forces to create a forensic lab.[10] A 2017 business plan for Transforming Forensics

---

[9] J.J. Koehler and S. Liu, 'Fingerprint Error Rate on Close Non-matches', *Journal of Forensic Sciences* 66(1) 129–134 (2021). Available at https://doi.org/10.1111/1556-4029.14580.

[10] 'Lancashire Police Teams up with Four Forces in Forensic Science Deal', *BBC News* (20 September 2021). Available at https://www.bbc.co.uk/news/uk-england-lancashire-58623627.

was already talking about rapid DNA testing at crime scenes within three to five years.[11] As far-fetched as that may seem right now, the intention behind it isn't, and technology will soon allow it to happen.

Amidst this, the Forensic Science Regulator (FSR) has pushed for accreditation of most areas of forensics. External assessments of any kind should improve quality, but they also raise costs. At the moment, accreditation is not mandatory, but this is changing. As I write this, a Bill to give the FSR statutory power has passed the House of Commons and the House of Lords and is in its final stages.[12]

Where does that leave defence experts?

The FSR has maintained—and I would agree in principle—that defence experts should be included in a quality structure, which should check for competence, consistency and require a peer-review for all reports. There are various ways this can be done, but only one, under United Kingdom Accreditation Service (UKAS) accreditation to ISO 17025 or 17020, has been permitted.

Most defence experts are sole providers or employed by small to medium companies. Accreditation is based on the methods used and not company size, making the cost per head far higher for small businesses. Legal Aid for those doing defence work remains lower than the rate they were allowing at the turn of the millennium.

More importantly, does accreditation truly improve quality? In that sense, I don't know if anyone has studied this. There are already a few accredited methods in use for criminal work that are not fit for purpose. For example, pH paper is accredited for use to report critical findings in criminal matters (such as assaults using corrosive liquids), despite the

---

[11] *Transforming Forensics: Outline Business Case*, Home Office National Police Chiefs' Council (31 March 2017). Available at https://www.npcc.police.uk/2017%20FOI/CO/078%2017%20 CCC%20April%202017%2008%20Transforming%20Forensics%20Business%20Case%20 March%202017.pdf.

[12] Forensic Science Regulator Act 2021. Available at https://www.legislation.gov.uk/ukpga/ 2021/14/contents.

fact the pH paper is insensitive and involves a degree of subjectivity in reading the colour. Accurate pH meters have been available for decades, but accreditation is about writing procedures and following them, not necessarily about whether the procedures themselves are best practice.

My main concern is that over the last 30 years, I have seen no real change in the reasons *why* cases fall off the rails. It's not because of bad science or scientists, bad methods, or a lack of accreditation. Quite the opposite: labs have always had competent people, and well-documented and robust methods underpinned by validation studies, even before ISO 17025 was applied. The methods many labs use today are no different from the ones being used 20–30 years ago. Not surprisingly, the scientific findings are usually correct.

The problems we encounter as defence experts have largely to do with contextual considerations, the effects of cognitive bias, and a lack of joined-up thinking. The push for accreditation won't change that, and the criminal justice system needs truly reliable independent experts capable of thinking outside the box in order to spot errors.

However, if a defence expert, who lacks accreditation, doesn't agree with the Crown's expert, who has it, the prosecution will argue that their expert is better purely by virtue of this, regardless of the core issues with the reliability of the evidence. It just happened to a colleague of mine— and accreditation isn't even mandatory yet.

Once a few cases like this go forward, barristers or the courts might demand only accredited experts. If we continue down this path with no change, the criminal justice system will see an erosion of defence experts, lost in a sea of expensive bureaucracy that has forced them to abandon ship.

The absence of a defence expert runs the risk of expert interpretation ending up in the hands of lawyers and jurors, who might not spot the critical failings that only an expert can see. Paradoxically, the altruistic idea of getting every forensic expert (be they prosecution or defence) to the same mandatory quality standard could lead to the scales of justice being tipped very much in favour of the prosecution.

A defence expert is the last technical check in the criminal process, and their role is critical in helping to prevent miscarriages of justice. The work is interesting, varied, and sometimes breaks a case open in a way that the detective TV shows suggest happens every time. But if you are a forensic expert who is thinking of crossing to the dark side, you might want to shine a light in first and make sure you aren't stepping off a cliff.

Index

Me circa 1992 at Keith Borer Consultants, Durham in admin. Reports were dictated or handwritten and handed over to be written up.

Massachusetts, USA 1998, back at Quincy, PD with two detectives having wrapped up at a crime scene.

Hurricane Ivan Sept 11, 2004—Ocean Club with it's beautiful ocean view in the background. We owned it for 5 days before the hurricane replaced the downstairs kitchen, lounge (with furniture) and the walls with a large lump of coral.

Fire investigation in the Cayman Islands, 2014, with borrowed bunker gear from the airport crew.

www.ingramcontent.com/pod-product-compliance
Lightning Source LLC
Chambersburg PA
CBHW071741270326
41928CB00013B/2754